WHERE
NO ONE
HAS
HEARD

"*Where No One Has Heard* takes us on a journey of a remarkable life with a wonderful family background and an immeasurable legacy of impact on the lives of others—including my own. My vision for missions and commitment to pray for the nations came through the influence of my seminary professor, Dr. J. Christy Wilson. And his well-recorded story here will have the same impact on you! Dr. Wilson's life will challenge you, encourage you, and stimulate you to discover God's unique purpose for your life and your role in global missions."

—Paul Borthwick, Development Associates International;
author, *A Mind for Missions* and *Western Christians in Global Mission*

"Ken Wilson's book *Where No One Has Heard* is the powerful story of a missionary statesman. It is the story of J. Christy Wilson's journey with Jesus Christ as he immersed himself in family life, in educational pursuits, in world evangelization ministry, in dangerous moments, and in dying. I could not put the book down once I had started reading it. Neither will most readers! The chapters dealing with Christy and Betty Wilson's time in Kabul, Afghanistan, are a record of faithful and dedicated ministry, along with passionate care and concern for the Afghans. The narrative of their ministry and influence at Gordon-Conwell Theological Seminary is a record of effective teaching and learning. Students' lives were transformed! He was the Michelangelo of educators. I can personally testify to Christy's spiritual disciplines: Bible reading and memorization, personal evangelism, fasting, and moment-by-moment prayer—a profound influence, indeed. It was always about Christ!"

—Robert E. Cooley, president emeritus,
Gordon-Conwell Theological Seminary

"An inspiring glimpse at the life of a missions leader who helped launch a movement mobilizing generations of students into God's global mission. *Where No One Has Heard* is a powerful reminder of what God can do through anyone willing to surrender his or her own life."

—Tom Lin, president and CEO of InterVarsity
Christian Fellowship; director of Urbana '15

"A truly inspirational and well-written biography. I had tears in my eyes at several points because it captured the man so well. I am very impressed with this work."

—Timothy C. Tennent, president and professor of world Christianity, Asbury Theological Seminary

"Packed with inspiring accounts of how hundreds of Afghans and Christian workers around the world were impacted by Christy Wilson's life, prayers, and love for Jesus. It will impact you as it did me."

—J. Dudley Woodberry, interim pastor (1971–72) and pastor (1974–76), Community Christian Church of Kabul; dean emeritus, School of Intercultural Studies, Fuller Theological Seminary

"Christy Wilson had a profound impact upon Christian missions, Afghanistan, and a generation of students at Gordon-Conwell Theological Seminary. Ken Wilson compellingly tells the story of this man who loved Christ, the people who loved Christ, and those who had not yet embraced his Savior. This book will be an inspiration to faithfully respond to Christ's Great Commission."

—Dennis P. Hollinger, president and Colman M. Mockler Distinguished Professor of Christian Ethics, Gordon-Conwell Theological Seminary

"As a former student of Christy Wilson, I observed him from a distance with a sense of awe and respect. He was known, among all students, as a man whose life was absorbed in bringing glory to his Lord. Now, Ken Wilson has skillfully brought Christy Wilson 'to life' with his humble, respectful, and meaningful biography. I could not put the book down, absorbed as I was in the telling of this story. But in the end, I did not walk away praising Christy Wilson, or Ken Wilson, but God, who made that life possible."

—Jeffrey Arnold, pastor and author, *The Big Book on Small Groups*

"The Christy Wilson story is a must-read for all who want to be inspired by a man of God who lived a life of prayer and purpose. Ken has beautifully written on one of my former mission professors and heroes of the faith. I feel a great sense of awe and respect as I sit in the office as the director of the J. Christy Wilson, Jr. Center for World Missions. Thank you, Ken, for sharing with us this precious treasure; Christy was a man who exemplified a humble, sacrificial missionary spirit with a heart for God and a love for the Afghan people."

—David Ro, director of the J. Christy
Wilson, Jr. Center for World Missions

Where No One Has Heard is the story of a lifetime! A rollicking adventure of a brave and brilliant man driven by love—love of a people; love of a woman; and above all, love for his God. Ken Wilson has knit together amazing and important details of the life of J. Christy Wilson to give us, in full, the true story of a disciple of Christ many of us have only known in part. Wilson begins with the building blocks of faith from Dr. Wilson's childhood and upbringing as the foundation upon which the gospel is brought to a lost people. Along the way, we encounter daring rescues, dramatic conversions, political intrigue, kings and princes, demon possession, wealth and poverty, heartbreak, overwhelming joy, and most of all, story upon story of people from all walks of life coming to faith in Jesus Christ through the witness of this man of prayer and conviction. This is a story worth reading of a life well lived."

—Ivan S. Chow, Gordon-Conwell '92;
compiler, *More to Be Desired Than Gold*

"I could not put this down. I read it in two sittings. I would have read straight through, but LIFE interrupted! I laughed, cried, and felt challenged, motivated, and encouraged to move forward in my walk with Christ!"

—Gina Bolton, middle school teacher and pastor's wife

WHERE
NO ONE
HAS
HEARD

THE LIFE OF J. CHRISTY WILSON JR.

KEN WILSON

WILLIAM CAREY
LIBRARY

Scripture quotations are taken from the Holy Bible, New Living Translation, copyright ©1996, 2004, 2007, 2013, 2015 by Tyndale House Foundation. Used by permission of Tyndale House Publishers, Inc., Carol Stream, Illinois 60188. All rights reserved.

Published by William Carey Library
1605 E. Elizabeth St.
Pasadena, CA 91104 | www.missionbooks.org
Joanne Leong, graphic design

William Carey Library is a ministry of
Frontier Ventures
www.frontierventures.org

Printed in the United States of America

20 19 18 17 16 5 4 3 2 1 BP300

Library of Congress Cataloging-in-Publication Data
Names: Wilson, Ken, 1957- author.
Title: Where no one has heard : the life of J. Christy Wilson, Jr. / by Ken Wilson.
Description: Pasadena, CA : William Carey Library, 2015. | Includes bibliographical references and index.
Identifiers: LCCN 2015037890| ISBN 9780878086313 (pbk. : alk. paper) | ISBN 9780878088942 (ebook) | ISBN 0878086315 (pbk. : alk. paper)
Subjects: LCSH: Wilson, J. Christy, 1921-1999. | Christian biography.
Classification: LCC BR1725.W525 W55 2015 | DDC 266.0092 [B] --dc23 LC record available at https://lccn.loc.gov/2015037890

To Mimi—
my sweetheart, my best friend, my beloved bride,
my chief encourager in writing and in life

CONTENTS

FOREWORD

A wise person once said that the sign of a truly great life is not merely someone who does great things, but someone who enables others to do great things. If this is true, then J. Christy Wilson Jr. was one of the most profound examples of a truly great life. From the day I first met Christy Wilson, I found my life changed just from being with him. He always inspired me to pray more, to give more, to sacrifice more, to love more. But, as this book so nobly sets forth, this is not an experience limited to me, or even to a generation of students from Gordon-Conwell who are serving all over the world. This is the legacy of the life of J. Christy Wilson Jr. His influence was global, and it continues to the present. I have had the privilege of meeting people all over the world who were profoundly changed by their encounter with this godly man of faith and prayer. In fact, to meet someone who knew "Dr. Wilson" inevitably leads to the sharing of stories, testimonies, and memories, all pointing to his vibrant faith and his love for Christ, and joyfully remembering that infectious laugh of his that we all had grown to love.

In honor of Christy Wilson's seventieth birthday, a former student of his, Ivan Chow, gathered together a collection of stories told by Dr. Wilson in his classes and published them under the title *More to Be Desired Than Gold*. These were beloved stories, and all those who knew him cherished having them brought together into one place. I required this book for all my students during my years teaching at Gordon-Conwell. What is not widely known is that Dr. Wilson refused to receive any royalties for the book. Instead, all the proceeds of the book went to support a foundation that funded missionary work around the world. To the end, he was always leveraging his life for the kingdom.

Ken Wilson has now performed a great service by writing the first full-length biography of the life of J. Christy Wilson Jr. From the moment I heard about this project, I was an enthusiastic supporter, because I knew that it would be the catalyst that would introduce a new generation to the life and faithfulness of this beloved man and his dear wife, Betty. For those of us who knew him, we all remember how much he loved missionary biographies. It was in his classes years ago that I first read such classics as *Through Gates of Splendor* and *To the Golden Shore*. It is therefore a fitting tribute that we now have a missionary biography of the life of J. Christy Wilson Jr. May it inspire a new generation of Christians to bring the hope of Christ "where no one has heard."

Timothy C. Tennent

president and professor of world Christianity

Asbury Theological Seminary

PREFACE

"Who are the Christians in your life who you most respect?" The question jolted my mind from a meandering path of daydreams during our pastor's sermon. It jerked me back to full attention, much like a poke in the stomach might do. *Who are the Christians in my life who I most respect?* With little effort, three people immediately surfaced within my mind.

The first is a UPS-driver-turned-local-church-pastor, Wayne Schar, with whom I have shared ministry for about twenty years.

The second is a Russian orphan ministry leader, Yulia, whom I know from three short-term mission trips to the dilapidated but lively orphanage in Komsomolsk, Russia.

And the third is a professor of world evangelization at Gordon-Conwell Theological Seminary, J. Christy Wilson Jr., whose life briefly intersected with mine thirty years ago.

The common thread among these three saints is a life consumed with prayer, a joyful countenance even amid the most trying circumstances, and a love for the Lord Jesus Christ that overflows to anyone who dares to get near them.

After writing two books, the idea of writing a biography slowly settled in my mind. And the person who most intrigued me was Christy Wilson. I was a student in two of his classes (Personal Evangelism and World Missions), and my strongest personal recollections of him include the following:

- He wrote me a letter dated April 16, 1982, four months before I began seminary, in response to a letter I had written to him. I have no idea how I even knew of him, but he was the only professor to whom I wrote, and he responded with a most gracious typed letter accompanied by a handwritten reference to 1 Thessalonians 5:24.

- He provided a workshop on spiritual gifts for the entire seminary community. That evening I first learned of the concept of spiritual gifts, and I discovered that mine might be encouragement and evangelism.
- He counseled me one afternoon when I was struggling with what ministry and career path might best suit my unique gifts and bents. I don't recall him guiding me in any particular direction, but I do remember him praying for me.
- We encountered each other in a grocery store in Gloucester, Massachusetts. When I shared with him my excitement about a high school student in my youth group who had just given his life to Christ, he gently placed his hand on my shoulder (a common pose for Christy Wilson) and prayed for this new Christ follower, right there in the middle of the produce aisle.

Our lives intersected for only two years, and our paths seldom crossed during that time. Yet his influence upon me was indelible.

In recent years I have stumbled upon many tidbits of information about his life. The more I discover about this tender yet tenacious man of God, the more it seems that he was an Indiana Jones of the Christian faith. He was born and raised in Tabriz, Persia (now known as Iran); ran cross country and was captain of varsity track at Princeton University; helped launch what became the triennial Urbana missions conference; pioneered Christian work in Afghanistan, entering the country as one of only a few Christians in a nation of approximately twelve million Muslims; taught private English lessons to the crown prince; faced danger on numerous occasions; and pastored the only Christian church permitted on neutral soil in the entire nation of Afghanistan.

During the past several years, I have been privileged to interview many of Christy Wilson's surviving family members, including his younger sister, his wife, and his three children. I have also interviewed ministry colleagues and countless people whom he mentored and helped launch into ministries throughout the world.

Like all people, he had struggles and flaws accompanying his talents and gifts. I do not seek to mask my deep respect for this godly man of kindness and prayer (two qualities that I most remember in him, and two qualities he possessed more than anyone else I have ever known). However, I have tried not to elevate him onto a literary pedestal or paint him as a plaster saint, for that would be a disservice both to him and to you, the reader.

Some of the stories remain in Christy's own words because of the value and skill of his storytelling. And just in case you are wondering about our common last name, my only relationship to Christy Wilson is that of a brother in Christ.

Where No One Has Heard is a love story—primarily between a man and his God, but also between a man and his wife and children and between a man and a group of people he had not yet met.

I consider myself greatly privileged to write the first biography of Christy Wilson, and I do so with the prayer that it will challenge and inspire many to a life of greater love and ministry for the Lord, and that a new generation of personal evangelists, missionaries, prayer warriors, and Christ followers will follow in his footsteps. I also pray that you will gain a greater vision of the splendor of God, the wonder of the gospel, the power of prayer, the joys of following Christ, and the difference just one surrendered and exchanged life can make in this world.

Ken Wilson
Zelienople, Pennsylvania
November 2016

INTRODUCTION

God used J. Christy Wilson Jr. as a trailblazer in Afghanistan for our generation as he sought to follow in the steps of his Master. Then through his students he reached the world. Other Christians had made trails through Afghanistan in previous generations, but there was scarcely a trace of these after 1896 when the Armenians in Kabul left, with some going to Calcutta and Dhaka and others to Peshawar.

In 1971, as the War of Independence was breaking out, which led to East Pakistan becoming Bangladesh, Christy and I visited the Armenian monastery in Dhaka, where we gathered information on the Armenians of Kabul. We learned of three thieves who tried to steal the chalice and the candlestick holders from the altar of the Armenian Orthodox Church there. When they tried to climb a rope with their loot, they fell three times. Convinced that God was after them, they begged for baptism. They were called "the first fruits" of the mission, but few followed them. The Armenian Church, which was by the Bala Hissar Fortress, was largely destroyed in 1879 when an ammunition magazine exploded.

Earlier Christians had reached this Central Asian region by the fourth century. A bishop of Herat attended the Council of Seleucia in AD 424, and bishops and metropolitans were associated with that city until the eleventh century. But the massacres of Timur and Genghis Khan and Islamization eliminated most of the Christians by the fifteenth century. In the early 1970s, my wife, Roberta, and I visited a grave near Herat where Muslims went to pray, believing that it was the grave of a disciple of Jesus; but it could well have been the grave of a Christian from one of these earlier periods. There are reports of a Georgian bishop in Kabul in the fifteenth or sixteenth century, a Jesuit mission in the early 1600s, and even some Christian tribes in Kafiristan ("land of the disbelievers"), now called Nuristan ("land of light").

Armenian Christians moved to Herat, Kandahar, and Kabul, where in the latter part of the 1700s they probably built the church that was largely destroyed in 1879 and abandoned in 1896. There are occasional reports of itinerant preachers, such as Joseph Wolf, the first modern Westerner to preach there, in 1821 and in 1831–34. Since there was a government ban against conversion in Afghanistan, mission organizations such as the Church Missionary Society built missions stations with hospitals, schools, and churches just outside the porous borders of the country, such as in Peshawar. At All Saints Church there (where eighty-seven parishioners were killed and 170 were injured in 2013), there is a list of Afghan martyrs from 1858 to 1934.[1]

Here this biography picks up the story. When five-year-old Christy Jr. was being raised by missionary parents in Iran, he heard that Afghanistan next door was closed to evangelism; so he said, "I want to be a missionary to Afghanistan." We are led through his educational, character, and spiritual development in Iran, Lawrenceville School, Princeton University, and Princeton Theological Seminary. Then, as he is ready to go to the land of his calling, he encounters a series of delays that in God's timing lead him to be better trained academically, to receive pastoral experience, to be able to recruit others to go to Afghanistan and around the world, and to find a Canadian kindergarten teacher named Betty to be his wife and lifelong companion.

When the Wilsons finally arrive in Afghanistan, we see them join with other Christians to blaze a new trail of Christian ministry.

---

1.   For historical sources on Christianity in Afghanistan, see the *Oxford Encyclopaedia of South Asian Christianity* (New Delhi: Oxford University Press, 2011), s.v. "Afghanistan," by J. D. Woodberry.

Christy is first assigned to teach many of the future leaders of Afghanistan in their formative high school years and then the crown prince. Next the Community Christian Church of Kabul is started in homes. Then the book describes the mushrooming of ministries to local needs—both among Afghans and Western hippies who passed through the country.

The account goes on to describe the receiving of permission from the Afghan government to construct a church building and the joyful laying of its cornerstone in 1971, a replica of which still sits on my desk with the words, "Jesus Christ Himself being the chief cornerstone." The Wilsons then went on furlough to the United States from 1971 to 1972. After they returned, there was enough government opposition to the church building that the Wilsons felt that they should leave Afghanistan. Subsequently the church building and the wall of the courtyard were torn down as parishioners served tea to the soldiers and workmen, some of whom had tears in their eyes.

Next we are led through Christy's expanded ministry at Gordon-Conwell Theological Seminary, where he equipped students to serve around the world. In all of this, his motivation was perhaps best expressed by the song he asked my wife, Roberta, to sing at his funeral, "My Jesus, I Love Thee," which includes, "I love Thee in life; I will love Thee in death." That love has continued to motivate the many Afghan and expatriate workers and martyrs who have followed Christy and Betty in that land, for they all have followed the path of the one with nail prints in his feet.

J. Dudley Woodberry
interim pastor (1971–72) and pastor (1974–76),
Community Christian Church of Kabul
dean emeritus,
School of Intercultural Studies, Fuller Theological Seminary

It was the only Christian church building permitted on neutral soil in Afghanistan, constructed following a personal assist from President Eisenhower. The Afghan government permitted this place of worship only for use among the foreign community; it was never to be used by the Afghan people.

One Sunday morning, only three years after the sanctuary's dedication, soldiers arrived and began to hack away at the wall between the street and the church building.

One gentleman in the congregation went to Kabul's mayor and prophetically warned, "If your government touches that house of God, God will overthrow your government!" The mayor responded by ordering the congregation to turn over their church for destruction, thereby eliminating the need for the Afghan government to pay compensation.

"This building does not belong to us but to God," the people of the church replied. "We can't turn it over for destruction." And they proceeded to serve tea and cookies to the soldiers who were destroying their place of worship.

On Tuesday, July 17, 1973, the Afghan soldiers completed their destruction of the church building. That very night, King Mohammed Zahir Shah, who had ruled for forty years, was overthrown in a coup, and the 227-year-old monarchy in Afghanistan came to an end forever. The rest of that story is told in the history books.

The pastor of the only Protestant church in Afghanistan fell to the floor and wept. He had recently been pressured to leave Afghanistan, and as he departed the land and people he loved so much, he wiped the dust from his feet.

CHAPTER 1
FAMILY ROOTS

And through your descendants all the nations of the earth
will be blessed—all because you have obeyed me.
Genesis 22:18

The year was 1918. J. Christy Wilson (Sr.) had just obtained a crisp new ticket for passage on a ship preparing to cross the Atlantic Ocean. He was a passionate and ambitious Princeton student, eager to begin serving as a chaplain for the troops fighting in "the war to end all wars." However, on Monday, November 11, the day before he was to set sail, Germany signed an armistice in a railroad carriage in the French town of Compiègne. The Great War abruptly ended. And Christy's chance to serve was seemingly lost.

Most of the world greeted that historic day with an overwhelming sense of joy and relief. Christy Wilson was certainly among them. But now he also felt an unsettling blend of confusion and uncertainty. How could such timing have occurred? And now that he could no longer serve as a chaplain for the fighting soldiers, what would his immediate future hold?

One of Christy's classmates and friends at Princeton Theological Seminary, William Miller, hung a map of the world over his bed in his dormitory room to serve as a prayer guide. He would regularly kneel and pray, "Lord, I'll serve you anywhere in the world you want me to. Show me where you want me to go." Shortly after the armistice, sensing his friend's dismay, he approached Christy and said, "You're so disappointed you couldn't go overseas for your country. How about going overseas for your Lord?"

Christy and his new wife, Fern, soon joined the Student Volunteer Movement (SVM). Along with more than 100,000 other young people, they signed SVM decision cards that read "God helping me, I purpose to be a foreign missionary." They volunteered to go to Persia, Christy being the hundredth volunteer that William Miller had recruited for foreign missions. The following year, Christy, Fern, their young son Jack, and William departed together from New York. They were destined for the other side of the world, determined to bring Christ to the people of Persia.

Revolution was wreaking havoc in Russia as their ship crossed the Atlantic, passed through the Mediterranean Sea, and docked in Istanbul. Another ship transported them through the Black Sea to Russia. Finally, crossing several war zones, they journeyed by train and stagecoach until they reached their destination—Tabriz, Persia. Their journey from New York to their new home in Tabriz, close to Russia's southern border, had taken three months. Christy Wilson was just twenty-eight years old when he first arrived in Tabriz; he was to spend the next two decades of his life ministering in the land now known as Iran, the place where he would also raise his children.

• • •

J. Christy Wilson Sr. was born in Columbus, Nebraska, in 1891, the first son of Charles C. and Lillie Gray Moore Wilson. The initial "J." in his name was added as an afterthought: his father liked the way it looked in the signature. (Lillie wanted only the name Christy, but she decided that the "J." would be acceptable as long as it did not stand for Jay. While the signature may have looked attractive, the added initial caused considerable confusion in future years.)

Christy would grow up to be a strong Christian, with the defining mark of his life being a passion for the word of God. He was a dedicated and lively man who often had a twinkle in his blue eyes. Friends could tell when he was nearby, because he was usually whistling a tune, humming a song, or jingling his keys. When he needed to focus on something, he possessed an acute skill for tuning out everything around him.

One of Christy's early career ambitions was to be a sports broadcaster, and he played many sports as a child and young adult—baseball, football, tennis, and boxing. However, he also sensed a call into vocational ministry at a young age. During the hot summer months of 1914, after earning his bachelor's degree from the University of Kansas, Christy commenced two years of service as the newspaper editor for the *Daily Post* in Idaho Falls, Idaho. Finally, answering his call to ministry, he ventured east to New Jersey and enrolled at Princeton Theological Seminary.

During his years at Princeton, Christy had several professors who provided backbone to his faith and conviction to his theology. "They straightened me out," he later admitted. He had previously picked up liberal ideas, but these respected professors brought him to a thoroughly evangelical position. Benjamin B. Warfield and J. Gresham Machen left the most notable handprints upon the heart and mind of this young seminarian.

On July 19, 1918, Christy was ordained by the Lehigh Presbytery in the United Presbyterian Church, and a year later he received his two degrees from Princeton. 1919 was also the year in which he journeyed to Tabriz under the Presbyterian Board of Foreign Missions. While his primary ministry was that of an itinerant evangelist, his servant's heart also led him into a variety of other roles that others did not want. During a season of unusual suffering, Christy smuggled wheat across the Russian border to feed starving Armenians.

During Christy's twenty-two years in Persia, an unwritten agreement governed all mission ventures within the nation: the Presbyterians would minister in the northern part of Persia and the British Anglican mission society in the southern part. They worked closely together, and Christy headed up the mission collaboration in the Middle East. He also had the opportunity to participate in archaeological expeditions in the neighboring closed country of Afghanistan.

Christy loved fun. One of his hobbies was playing tennis, and he built a tennis court for the people of Tabriz. This peculiar game puzzled the Persians, however. They would sit and watch, confusion written on their faces. "Why do you waste your time chasing that little ball?" they asked. "Why don't you let your servants chase that ball and you sit and drink tea?"

In 1941, shortly after World War II had commenced, Christy began a twenty-year tenure as associate professor of missions and dean of field services at Princeton Theological Seminary. He followed in the large footsteps of Dr. Samuel Zwemer, his mentor and spiritual hero, who preceded him as professor of missions at Princeton. During his years on the faculty at Princeton Seminary, Christy authored several books and traveled with Dr. Frank Laubach's Literacy Campaign in Afghanistan as interpreter and linguistic aid. This relationship would play a vital role in the life of his second child, Christy Jr.

Throughout his years in Persia and at Princeton, Christy was blessed with a devoted partner in marriage and ministry. When he was a student at the University of Kansas, people kept telling Christy about a cute co-ed named Fern Wilson. "Is she your sister?" they would ask, curious about the common last name. "No," he would always reply. "But I'd better meet her," he sometimes threw in as an afterthought. He eventually looked her up, and the two fell in love soon after meeting.

J. Christy Wilson Sr. at the
University of Kansas
Courtesy of the Wilson family

Fern Wilson as a young mother in Persia
Courtesy of the Wilson family

Christy proposed to Fern by telegraph while he was at Princeton. After joyfully accepting, she traveled across the country to meet him in Washington, DC, where they were married. This was to be the beginning of a fifty-six-year partnership in marriage, missions, and ministry.

Fern Wilson was the youngest of eleven children, the daughter of a Civil War veteran father and a Cherokee mother. Like Christy, she was a strong Christian; she felt that her job in life was to pray, and it was this passion for prayer more than anything else that her children caught from her. She walked five miles on most days and would pray as she walked.

Fern had an uncommon gift of seeing into people's circumstances, traits, and character. She loved to sit at airports and watch people go by. "Children at home, more than one," she might say, and usually she was correct in her assessments. Perhaps as a counterpart to her sharp intuition, her speech could be cuttingly direct at times. She wasn't one to mince words with anyone, and this made her somewhat intimidating.

Fern's training in teaching and home economics served her well on the mission field of northern Persia: she was a good housekeeper, a good cook, and a good mother to her children. She also helped her husband with the mission work, teaching and working in the church. An unusual exchange of gifts reveals the playfulness and synergy of their partnership: Fern loved roses and knew how to take care of them, so for her birthday Christy would give her a bag of manure as fertilizer. For Christy's birthday, since he did the dishes after every meal, Fern would give him an apron.

Christy and Fern gifted the world with four children. Their first, Jack, was born while Christy was at Princeton, and was just a toddler when the family departed for Persia. Jack was never a good student and didn't graduate from high school. When he was old enough, he joined the army. Since they let him choose where he would be stationed, he asked for placement in Hawaii—but his timing was fateful: he found himself in Pearl Harbor on December 7, 1941. He served as a truck driver, and when the Japanese bombs began to fall from the skies, he hid underneath his truck.

Though unhurt in Pearl Harbor, Jack was shell-shocked from the Pacific island invasions. The war damaged him badly. He entered the army weighing 185 pounds but emerged a mere 125. He lost his teeth, his skin turned yellow due to malaria medication, and he couldn't even live in a house, ever fearful that it would be bombed. Jack was to live a very difficult life, eventually settling into a retirement home for veterans.

Christy Jr.'s younger brother, Stanley, was born in Persia in 1926. He was the most athletic in the family, playing tennis, golf, and any other sport he could find. Stanley spent three years in Iran, working in a sports program for people in the oil industry, before returning to the United States to continue his athletics career in California.

The youngest child, Nancy, was born in Persia in 1928. She and her husband had five children, and in addition to teaching junior high math, she worked in the church, teaching Sunday school, working with youth groups, and serving at church camps.

Fern and Christy's second child was J. Christy Jr. Like his father, Christy Jr. would serve as a Christian teacher and pastor in a Muslim nation for twenty-two years; he would apply to serve as a chaplain in a World War only to see it end before he could begin; and he would enjoy a two-decade teaching position as a professor of missions. J. Christy Wilson Jr. would bring the good news of salvation and the love of Christ to a forbidden nation where no one had yet heard. This book tells the story of his life.

CHAPTER 2
A PERSIAN CHILDHOOD

Direct your children onto the right path, and when
they are older, they will not leave it.
Proverbs 22:6

J. Christy Wilson Jr. was born on November 7, 1921, the lunar celebration of Muhammad's birthday, in the city of Tabriz, the second largest in Persia. Throughout his life, he carried with him a wealth of joyful memories from his childhood there.

Christy was surrounded by powerful witnesses from a young age. First and foremost were his parents. Each morning Christy's father led the family in devotions after breakfast, along with the servants, speaking in the servants' native tongue, Azerbaijani. Before breakfast they also recited a Psalm in English, enabling the children to memorize several Psalms. A reward from their father—usually a coin or a flower or anything else he could muster—awaited those who successfully memorized and recited Bible verses.

Every morning, Christy's father led his family in a simple child's prayer:

> Lead us, Dear Savior, through this day.
> Help us to love You and obey.
> Accept our thanks for all Your care.
> Bless our dear ones everywhere.
> Forgive our sins and hear our prayer.
> In Jesus' name, Amen.

Christy's parents also prayed with him at bedtime, and he soon started praying simple prayers on his own. The Lord's Prayer particularly struck him. Christy loved to emphasize the words "the power" at the close of that prayer.

Christy praying with a friend
in Persia at age two
Courtesy of the Wilson family

The local community of Christ followers in Persia also left an indelible mark on Christy's young heart and faith. There were over a hundred Presbyterian missionaries in northern Persia at that time, and the Muslim converts numbered over three thousand throughout the country. Since few missionary children had any real aunts or uncles living nearby, all of the missionaries became their adoptive aunts and uncles. The families enjoyed singing hymns in their homes, each person choosing a favorite hymn for all to sing.

The local congregation was distinctly international. One member of the congregation, a British banker, married the daughter of a local missionary. One day he diplomatically approached Christy's father, who served as their pastor, about the wording of the Lord's Prayer, which included the Presbyterian form, "Forgive us our debts." "Oh, as a banker, I just can't say that," he protested. "I much prefer 'Forgive us our trespasses'!"

Christy with the daughter
of missionary friends
Courtesy of the Wilson family

Christy's father loved having people from various backgrounds—Muslim, Jewish, Armenian, and Nestorian converts—all take communion together. At a very early age Christy learned to embrace people from different races, cultures, and languages, accepting them the way they were. He learned a variety of languages during his childhood, including Latin, French, and German in school, and Azerbaijani Turkish and some Russian through daily interactions with his friends.

Christy was greatly affected by the testimonies of the many Muslim converts he met during his childhood years. One such Muslim, Shamuel Nabi, experienced a glorious conversion through the witness of Christy's father. Shortly after Shamuel's conversion, Christy accompanied his father to visit Shamuel in the Tabriz Army Hospital. After a brief time of conversation with Christy and his father, Shamuel asked all the others in the ward to keep quiet while Christy's father led in prayer. This experience left a lasting impression upon the four-year-old Christy.

During Christy's childhood in Persia, as it is today in that part of the world, Muslims who came to Christ faced severe opposition both from family members and from society. Muslim law states that anyone who leaves Islam should be killed. Christy remembered some of the Muslim converts giving their lives for Christ as martyrs.

The Wilson home was open to many visitors over the years. Among them were Dr. Samuel Zwemer, one of history's foremost missionaries within the Muslim world; Dr. Robert Wilder, the founder of the Student Volunteer Movement; and Dr. Donald G. Barnhouse, a leading pastor from Philadelphia. Dr. Barnhouse, affectionately called Barney, had been a classmate of Christy's father, and young Christy was impacted by his preaching on salvation by faith.

Sunday school at the local church in Tabriz also helped shape young Christy's life and character. The Ten Commandments were written on the wall at the front of the church, capturing his attention on several occasions when he was six years old. During Sunday school, he tried to be clever by asking challenging questions. He once attempted to stump one of his teachers by asking why Jesus said "*This day* shalt thou be with me in paradise" if he was going to be in the grave for three.

Another Sunday school teacher, Clement Hydenburk, encouraged his students to memorize large portions of Scripture. Christy memorized such chapters as Matthew 5, Isaiah 53, and Psalm 42, and had to recite some of them in front of the parents. He frequently went to the "Inquirers' Room" at their church with his father, and he remembered watching blind Muslim converts read from their braille Bible. When Christy was twelve, he invented a Bible game with his younger brother, Stan, and their friends. Someone would read a passage from the Bible, and then everyone else had to find the corresponding book, chapter, and verse. Christy usually found it in little time, and he seldom lost.

Wilson family in Persia (Christy on back left)
Courtesy of the Wilson family

Christy's father once mentioned to him that he had read the entire New Testament by the time he was twelve years old. Christy decided, then and there, that he was better than his father and would read the entire New Testament before he was eleven. His determination to surpass his father's example, along with the example of his older brother, Jack, in reading his Bible in the mornings, launched Christy into daily devotions, a discipline that he carried on throughout his life.

The Wilson family also read books together, and one particular book—*The Story of a Bad Boy*—shaped young Christy in an unusual way. The book mentioned that the bad boy thought he was the greatest person on earth if people would only realize it. At the time, young Christy felt the same way about himself. It was one of his first glimpses into the pride of the human heart.

While Christy was becoming aware of his own fallenness, a powerful yet simple message was gently making its way into his heart:

> God loves us. He loves us completely; he loves us passionately. The Maker of the universe carefully crafted us, and he delights in us.
>
> However, our lives consistently miss the mark of God's holiness, and the Bible calls this sin. Because of our sin, we are all spiritually bankrupt and eternally separated from God. We are utterly powerless to make ourselves right with God by any good works or religious credentials. We can never be good enough to earn our way into heaven.
>
> In his great love for us, however, God sent his Son, Jesus, who shed his blood and died on the cross to pay the penalty for our sin. His death purchased our salvation and ransomed us back to God. Christ alone is perfectly holy, Christ alone rose from the dead, and Christ alone is able to restore us to God.
>
> To be reconciled to God and to know him personally, we must turn from our sin and put our trust in Jesus as the one who paid the penalty for our sin. We must personally accept Christ and his free gift of salvation. When we do, we become a new creation. God gradually transforms our life here on earth through his indwelling Holy Spirit and gives

us the assurance of eternal life with him in heaven, all for his own glory.[1]

As early as Christy could remember, this gospel message gripped his heart and Christ was his Savior. During his parents' second furlough, when he was eleven years old, he made his first public confession of faith. Christy would later write a twenty-page spiritual autobiography hidden away in the back portion of a personal journal, including the following account of his spiritual conversion:

> As to the actual time of my conversion, I do not remember any one definite experience. But I know that when I joined the First Presbyterian Church of Princeton, N.J. in 1933 under Dr. Charles Erdman, I made a profession of my faith in Christ openly and also believed in my heart. With my family living in the Princeton missionary apartments, one lady from the Belgian Congo started a Christian club for us children. Her name was Mrs. Mott Martin and the club was called the I.A.H. club. These letters stood for I Am His. After instruction, those of us who accepted Christ indicated it and thus received a silver ring to wear with these initials on it.

Not only did Christy's faith in Christ take root at an early age, but his life calling was also implanted within his heart as a young boy. When Christy was just five years old, Pastor Stefan Huviar, the beloved Nestorian evangelical pastor who labored alongside Christy's father in Tabriz, asked Christy what he wanted to do when he grew up. Christy had frequently heard his parents praying for Afghanistan, an unreached country to the east. He knew that this country, approximately the size of Texas, didn't have one Christian.

---

1. This explanation of the gospel is in the author's own words, but it is based on Scripture and Christy's teachings.

"I want to be a missionary to Afghanistan," Christy informed Pastor Huviar.

"Well," the pastor responded, "missionaries aren't allowed in Afghanistan."

"That's why I want to be one there," Christy immediately replied.[2] As he grew older, this sense of calling would germinate and blossom into his life's passion.

During his fourteen years in Persia, Christy picked up a wide assortment of hobbies. Among his favorites, and one that was particularly popular with his Persian playmates, was flying pigeons. Christy raised the pigeons himself and flew them every morning and evening. When he and his friends went on hikes, he sometimes took a pigeon along with him and tied a little message to its foot; when he threw the pigeon up into the air, it flew to the Wilson home and personally delivered the message to his mother. Christy's homing pigeons served as a favorite means of communication.

He and his friends also enjoyed flying kites. Christy made his own, one of which had a long tail and a Chinese lantern with a candle in it. When he flew it in the dark, people from far away could see it bobbing up and down against the backdrop of the Persian night sky.

When he was eight years old, Christy learned how to make a Persian rug from a local artisan. "I'm going to Princeton when I'm older," Christy informed his instructor, "so I'm stitching the team mascot, a tiger, into my rug."

"Most rugs don't have animals in them," noted the rug maker. Nevertheless, Christy persisted and made an eighteen-by-thirty-inch rug, possibly the only Persian rug ever made with a tiger on it.

Christy enjoyed hiking, particularly with the Boy Scouts. During one of his parents' furloughs in Princeton, the local Boy Scout troop bent the official rules for Christy, letting him join at age eleven rather than the normal twelve, realizing that he would soon

---

2. Interestingly, although this story was frequently retold by Christy's mother, he himself did not remember the conversation.

be returning to his home in Persia. He was grateful to continue his scouting career in Persia as well, where many of his hikes with his father included archaeological digs for ancient artifacts.

Christy's childhood education included homeschooling through sixth grade, a year in Princeton's public school during a family furlough, and a year with his younger brother, Stan, at a new school in Tehran, four hundred miles from their home in Tabriz.

When Christy was fourteen years old and about to enter high school, his parents faced a difficult decision. There were no opportunities for a high school education in Persia at that time. Assessing the situation, they sensed that they had three alternatives. One was to send their children back to the United States alone. However, this would make it appear that their parents didn't love them. A second was to send Fern back to the United States with the children, but this would make it look as if Christy's father didn't love his wife or his children. Finally, the entire family could return—but this might lead people to think that Christy's parents didn't love the Lord because they'd gone back on their call.

In 1936, at great sacrifice, they made the decision for Fern to return with her four children. Christy's father remained on the mission field without them for more than three years. It was not until late 1939, when World War II erupted, that he returned to the United States and was reunited with his family.[3]

As Christy's mother prepared to bring the children to the United States to continue their education, his father drafted a letter to a preparatory school in Lawrenceville, New Jersey, requesting a scholarship. They wrote back asking, "What proof do you have that you need a scholarship for your son?"

"Well, my missionary salary for a family of six for a whole year," he replied, "is less than what you charge for tuition, room, and board for one student for nine months."

---

3. Christy would later say that he thought his parents had made the wrong decision and that they should have returned to the United States as a whole family.

Christy left his childhood home of Persia at the age of four-teen and enrolled at Lawrenceville School near Princeton. He was equipped with a full scholarship of $1,500 per year for the next four years, as well as a heart full of anticipation.

CHAPTER 3
BLOSSOMING IN
PRINCETON AND
EDINBURGH

Work hard so you can present yourself to God and receive
his approval. Be a good worker, one who does not need to be
ashamed and who correctly explains the word of truth.
2 Timothy 2:15

During his school years in the United States, Christy faced many new challenges to his fledgling faith in Christ. The first battle of heart and spirit came during his very first morning as an American student. Christy was a high school freshman at Lawrenceville School in central New Jersey, and the year was 1936. As he later described, "On arriving in Lawrenceville, I had a little 'cube' in a dormitory of about 35 boys, called Ross House. It was a real battle the first morning I was there to read my Bible since our cubes were open and others could see what I was doing. But after an inward struggle, the Lord gave me grace to do it. From then on I would wake up early each morning for a devotional time."

Another challenge came from an unexpected source: the new teacher who was assigned to head up the Bible Department. He promptly changed the name to Religion Department and slowly took on a critical and philosophical approach. From his daily study of the Bible, Christy clearly recognized that the higher criticism being promoted did not hold water. He wrote an editorial for the school newspaper, the *Lawrence*, expressing his concerns about the new Religion Department, but since he also served as editor, he decided not to publish it.

Christy got into discussions and arguments with his classmates about the Bible. Although two of them seemed to be at least somewhat moved—a German foreign exchange student and the son of a Major League Baseball player—many showed no interest whatsoever. During his final year at Lawrenceville, Christy wanted to start a small prayer group, but he gave up the idea after no one responded to his invitations.

At one point Christy was asked to lead chapel. After prayer and scrapping one talk, he spoke about the three purposes people can have in life—some just live, some live for money and pleasure, but others live for Christ. Afterward Christy felt that the Lord had spoken through him and that his talk had made a significant impression. Several years later, he met a dying boy who mentioned his chapel talk from years past. Christy would later regret, however, that he didn't take advantage of the opportunity to press the salvation message home with that dying boy.

With Christy's mother alone with her four children in the United States while his father remained in Persia, the family spent summer vacations at missionary resorts such as Mountain Rest in Massachusetts, Chautauqua in New York, and Ventnor in New Jersey. The little church in Ventnor, St. John's by the Sea, possessed a warm evangelistic spirit that left a strong impression on young Christy—he found himself simultaneously put to shame by the boldness of the young people who gave testimonies and prayed out loud, something he was afraid to do at the time, and inspired by the many missionaries with whom he rubbed shoulders.

Christy's four years at Lawrenceville stretched not only his spiritual life but also his academic and vocational pursuits. At different times he contemplated becoming an archaeologist, a diplomat, or a missionary doctor. A four-hundred-question vocational test, however, revealed that he might be best suited for teaching math or science, becoming a YMCA director, or serving as a minister.

Outside the classroom, Christy was captain of both the soccer and track teams. His yearbook entry shows that he was selected as "Best All-Around Boy" in his house.

Entry for Christy Wilson in the Lawrenceville School yearbook
Courtesy of the Wilson family

In 1940, Christy graduated as valedictorian. Many years earlier his parents had purchased two Persian silk carpets, thinking they would one day finance their son's college education, but Christy's academic standing enabled him to obtain a scholarship to Princeton University, just six miles up the road from Lawrenceville. He waited on tables to pay for his room and board.

In planning his college curriculum, Christy initially worked out a pre-med schedule, but his father cautioned him that missionary doctors devote most of their time and energy to medical issues. He advised Christy that, if he sensed God's leading to work in Afghanistan, training in evangelistic work might be better than medical training. By the time he entered Princeton in the fall, Christy had decided to abandon the pre-med schedule and instead enroll in a bachelor of arts curriculum in the humanities. (He also requested an auto mechanics course, knowing that it would serve him well when he finally got to Afghanistan. His advisor, however, wouldn't allow it. "Oh, you're academic," he informed Christy, "and that's not the sort of thing you want to take.")

During Christy's first weeks at Princeton, a classmate invited him to a prayer meeting of the Princeton Evangelical Fellowship (PEF), held in one of the dormitory rooms. Thus began what proved to be Christy's most profitable spiritual help during his university years. Donald Fullerton, an alumnus from the class of 1912, taught the PEF Bible class on Sunday afternoons and invested greatly in Christy's life.

The men in PEF recruited Christy to help distribute copies of the Gospel of John to the entire freshman class. Christy was embarrassed at first, since the recipients were his own classmates, including many students he knew from Lawrenceville. However, he would later be grateful that he had persisted in the work. Twenty-six of his classmates were to die in World War II.

At the university, his French and history professors took particular delight in ridiculing Christianity and the Bible. Christy talked extensively with both professors but got nowhere. In the face of such opposition, he found that going straight to the Bible as the original source and fostering daily fellowship with other Christians kept his faith vibrant and strong.

Since Christy felt that God had used him as editor of the *Lawrence* during high school, he also considered joining the staff of the *Daily Princetonian*. In praying about the decision, he came across the verse in Jeremiah that says, "Cause me not to return to the house of . . . the scribe, lest I die there" (37:20). At first this seemed mere chance, and he continued pursuing a role with the newspaper. Later, however, he sensed that God had allowed him to be punished because he did not follow God's leading. He lost sleep while working nights at the newspaper, he lost money because the newspaper prevented him from waiting on tables at the commons, and he lost high grades in his academic pursuits. He also quickly found that many students working at the newspaper were immoral and foul-mouthed. On top of all this, the newspaper soon folded due to the Second World War. This experience taught Christy lifelong lessons about obeying God's guidance.

With the draft law taking all pre-ministerial students who weren't in seminary, Christy enlisted in the Army Enlisted Reserve. After just six months of service, however, the Lord showed him through the Scriptures and prayer that he wanted him to apply for a discharge. Having learned the bitter lesson of disobeying God before, he obeyed this time. In ways that seemed marvelous to Christy, at a time when the war was raging most violently in 1942, he was given an honorable discharge to continue his studies in preparation for the chaplaincy.

When Christy completed his application for service as a chaplain, his paperwork was returned to him with a request for a full first name. He resubmitted the application with the entry "J(only)," and his name was promptly registered as "Jonly Christy Wilson"—but the war ended before he could serve.

The Lord used Christy's obedience in leaving the army to resolve an area of discouragement in his life. As he reflected later, "One thing which became a real concern to me was that as far as I knew I had never been able to lead anyone to Christ. Right after obeying the Lord in the matter of getting out of the Army, I was privileged to lead John Morris, a classmate, to the Saviour. Then followed my brother Stanley and other classmates."

At this time, Christy also taught Sunday school at the nearby Jamesburg Reformatory. During his first year, his students were boys in the regular houses. During his second year, however, he taught the boys who were in confinement. Christy had glorious times being locked in with them on Sunday mornings, and he was privileged to lead two boys in the reformatory to Christ.

Christy ran cross country and was also captain of the varsity track team while at Princeton. His track career included a race in Madison Square Garden in which he received the winner's medal for the quarter mile. During his last year at the university, when over thirty students gave their lives to Christ, three of them were from the track team. (The Bible class led by Donald Fullerton, though it faced significant opposition, was a great spiritual help to the many new followers of Christ.)

Christy managed to excel in many areas despite his absent-mindedness. One day, after a track meet, he went to the university gymnasium to get his clothes out of the locker—only to be reminded that the gym had burned down earlier that year!

An annual tradition at Princeton was a one-mile relay race between classes, with gold medals donated by a wealthy alumnus for each winner. One year when Christy was chosen to serve as the anchor for his class team, he knew all too well that the last leg for a competing class, Skip Payne, was faster than he was.

Christy running a race on the Princeton track team
Courtesy of Archives of the Billy Graham Center, Wheaton, IL

When the race began, the first three sprinters on Christy's team gained a slight lead, and Christy received the baton a few feet ahead of Skip. He ran as fast as his feet would carry him, but as he approached the final stretch, he could hear Skip's pounding footsteps getting closer and closer. It appeared certain that Skip would reach the finish line first.

However, as Skip was passing Christy, he ran too close to his competitor, and Christy's right hand accidentally knocked Skip's baton to the ground. By the time he had retrieved it, Christy had already won the race. Feeling terrible about the outcome, Christy went to Skip's dorm room that evening and offered him the gold medal. Skip, however, refused to accept it. Christy then proceeded to tell Skip of an even greater race he could win, one with an eternal prize of far greater worth than any gold medal. They talked together, investigated key scriptures that reveal the gospel message, and finally prayed together as Skip placed his trust in Christ as his Savior. That night, due to an inadvertent bump of a baton, Christy led his track rival to become a follower of Christ.

One unrelated but noteworthy element of Christy's years at Princeton was occasional encounters with Albert Einstein, who lived on Mercer Street, just a few blocks from the Princeton campus. On the wall of the shoe store where Christy and Einstein both bought their shoes, Christy noticed a framed check signed by the scientist. He was told that Einstein had a terrible time balancing his checkbook, since so many people kept his personal checks in order to retain the genius' autograph.

With the war raging on, Christy had to continue his studies through the summer months. This enabled him to graduate early, in the fall of 1943. Since the Princeton Seminary term began several weeks before his graduation from the University, he was permitted to enroll simultaneously in both institutions for a brief period.

The transition from a secular university to a seminary was a breath of fresh air for Christy. His spiritual studies, once an extra-curricular endeavor, now became part of his regular curriculum. All of his classes were opened with prayer, and he felt privileged to live and study with a group of godly men. The residents of Brown Hall had nightly prayer meetings in each other's rooms, including prayer for their practical weekend work.

Christy's practical fieldwork while at Princeton included local church ministry with youth, InterVarsity Christian Fellowship (IVCF) work with college students, and a summer of missions work in New Mexico among the poor. While in New Mexico, Christy lived with the local people in their single-room homes. The bed bugs were relentless, but Christy was unwilling to get up or fight them off, because that would embarrass his hosts. So night after night he quietly lay there and let the bed bugs drink his blood. While Christy's fieldwork reports did not give him the highest marks for preaching, they generally commended him in the areas of personal character and evangelism. "He is not a particularly strong public speaker but a most Christlike person," one supervisor noted.

After completing his studies at Princeton, Christy heard that the Afghan government had openings for teachers. Early in 1947, he filled out the forms and applied to the Afghan Embassy in Washington, DC, for a position teaching English. But Christy heard nothing for more than six months, so as an alternate plan he decided to work on a PhD in Islamic studies at the University of Edinburgh.

During the eighteen months between Princeton and Edinburgh, two life-changing events would take place: while continuing his work with IVCF, Christy would launch a missions conference that continues to this day, one that has changed the face of world missions; and at that conference he would encounter a young Canadian kindergarten teacher, leading to a love story that would endure for half a century. These stories are chronicled in the next two chapters.

• • •

Christy quickly settled into life in his new surroundings in Edinburgh. His daily activities included a morning quiet time, ping pong, Arabic studies, afternoon bagpipes, and evening study by a fireplace, as illustrated in a letter that he wrote to his parents during his first semester as a doctoral student in Scotland. The letter included Christy's daily itinerary and a small descriptive sketch next to each time slot.

Christy's daily schedule in Edinburgh
Courtesy of Archives of the Billy Graham Center, Wheaton, IL

Christy wasted no time in joining an InterVarsity group that met on Friday nights in Edinburgh. Through this group he soon met Gwyn Walters, a classmate from Wales who would become a lifelong friend and fellow professor at Gordon-Conwell Theological

Seminary. Since the university did not provide dormitories at that time, students lived in private homes, and Christy lived in the home of an elderly woman named Mrs. Jarvis. Christy and Gwyn met together for prayer almost every day in a cobweb-filled room in one of the university buildings.

Gwyn once noted that Christy exhibited a "confluence of tenderness and tenacity" expressed within a diversity of settings. Christy sometimes played the role of the Pied Piper, marching his way over the hills and dales of Edinburgh, rhythmically gliding a violin bow over a hand saw to create ethereal tunes. Children fell in line to follow him, and Christy would eventually earn the right to share his faith in Christ with them.

During the summer of 1948, Christy spent several weeks with Gwyn in Wales. The two men led a group of young evangelical students, and together they would travel from village to village for a full week of meetings in each. If they were unable to return home in the evening on the local bus, they would often sleep in the church building.

During that same summer, the two comrades in ministry also traveled to the European continent. They made their way to a majestic alpine castle to participate in a conference for the International Fellowship of Evangelical Students (IFES). Christy met with many other young people, some of whom became Christian leaders for future generations. Among them was Dawson Trotman, the founder and leader of The Navigators. Together, Christy and "Daws" shared their visions for ministry, Christy to bring the gospel to the forbidden land of Afghanistan and Daws to reproduce disciples throughout the world.

Gwyn and Christy also journeyed to Geneva, Switzerland, to the church in which John Calvin had pastored during the 1500s. Gwyn stood at the foot of Calvin's pulpit, unable to bring himself to occupy the same lofty stature as his theological hero. His heart beat a little bit faster than usual, and his eyes scanned the swelling crowd of tourists that filled the historic church. Seizing the moment, Christy suggested to Gwyn, "Now you talk to the tourists about the gospel Calvin preached, and I'll pray in the back." Taking the pulpit, Gwyn proceeded to address the crowd.

While in Scotland, Christy befriended many other international students and saw that they were particularly receptive to the gospel. Dawson Trotman had taught him to prioritize disciple making as essential, so he prayed and chose seven students to mentor and meet with regularly. Christy's investment paid off in years to come—all seven of these men would be powerfully used by God in their home countries.

There were also times when one of his professors would commit an assortment of theological aberrations during a lecture. Most of Christy's classmates were afraid to challenge their teacher, knowing it could very well put their doctoral degree at risk. Christy, however, would raise his hand, stand up, and gently but uncompromisingly question the professor's assertions that failed to align with Scripture.

One of Christy's most memorable experiences during his doctoral studies was attending the 1948 Summer Olympics in London. He and Gwyn were present at the opening ceremony as the athletes entered Wembley Stadium for the traditional Parade of Nations, marching past King George VI and the royal family. The two friends watched eagerly as Olympians from each nation filed by—first the delegation from Greece, since the Olympics originated there, and then each nation in alphabetical order.

Following Greece, to Christy's astonishment, were athletes from Afghanistan. As they walked past, Christy was deeply moved; he was thrilled to discover that this isolated country would be part of the Olympics, but he also felt a burden to bring to them the message of salvation. He quietly asked God to show him some way to share the gospel with the Afghan athletes before they returned to their homeland.

When the ceremony had ended, Christy and Gwyn went to the British and Foreign Bible Society office. "Do you have any New

Testaments in Persian?" they asked, knowing that this was the closest language to Dari, the dialect of Persian spoken in Afghanistan.

As a matter of fact, they did.

"Could you possibly give a copy of the New Testament to each of the Afghan athletes?" the two men pressed further. "There are none available in their nation."

The Bible Society immediately embraced the idea, and they carried it even further: why not provide every Olympian with a New Testament in his or her native language? As a gesture of goodwill, they decided to stamp the book covers with the Olympic insignia in gold.

Since there were few security restrictions at that time, the Bible Society was able to enter the Olympic Village and distribute the New Testaments freely.

Years later, when Christy was teaching English in Kabul, a student asked him if they could talk after class. They strolled together through the school's garden, where there was more privacy. "I've been reading a very interesting book, and I wanted to ask you some questions about it," the student explained, reaching into his coat pocket. "My friend loaned it to me." In his hand he held a Persian New Testament. Its cover bore a familiar symbol: the Olympic rings in gold.

CHAPTER 4
LAUNCHING
A MISSIONS
CONFERENCE

But you will receive power when the Holy Spirit comes upon you. And you will be my witnesses, telling people about me everywhere—in Jerusalem, throughout Judea, in Samaria, and to the ends of the earth.
Acts 1:8

Christy's first contact with missions came even before his first words, his first steps, or his first friendships. His childhood home in Persia was a perpetual showcase displaying God's heart for missions.

However, his initial contact with InterVarsity Christian Fellowship (IVCF) came when he was a freshman at Princeton. It was a cool fall evening in 1940 when two young men, both unknown to Christy, paid an unexpected visit to his dorm room. David Adeney had served as a missionary to China and was now working with IVCF. His friend, Arthur Muller, was a seminary student and would later become a missionary to Iran. David asked Art if there were any Christian students at Princeton. Upon hearing Art's reply, the two made their way to find Christy. So began Christy's association with InterVarsity—an association that would leave an indelible imprint upon both.

Soon after, Christy first encountered Stacey Woods. InterVarsity/USA was a new ministry, and Stacey had recently taken the helm as their first secretary-general. The two IVCF pioneers met at a Victorious Life Conference in Keswick, New Jersey, in 1941, during the summer months between Christy's freshman and sophomore years. Stacey went to great lengths to share his vision for student evangelism with Christy, recognizing his Christian maturity and potential, and immediately had his eye on Christy for future involvement in IVCF. In turn, Christy quickly came to appreciate the work that Stacey was doing as the ministry was just beginning to blossom in the United States.

An influential IVCF board member, Mrs. F. Cliffe Johnston from New York, had been urging Stacey to find someone from an Ivy League college to serve on staff. In September 1943, Christy became that person. He initially joined staff on a part-time basis, working with InterVarsity on weekends while still a student at Princeton.

During Christy's early years with the ministry, he was responsible for visiting college campuses throughout New York and New England. His task was simply to pass along his passion for missions to other college students. Lacking a car of his own—and with very little money to his name—he traveled by train many weekends. When he became a seminary student, he was entitled to a clergy train pass; this provided him with both a reduced fare and a first-class ticket, and for an additional three dollars, it also entitled him to an upper berth in a more luxurious Pullman car.

Christy frequently traveled by train into New York City and then caught a sleeper car en route to Boston. When the train finally arrived the following morning, Christy would awake, shave along with the traveling salesmen who had taken the trip, and make his way to Harvard. One of his contacts was Dr. Harold John Ockenga, pastor of Park Street Church in downtown Boston. Dr. Ockenga was highly supportive of InterVarsity and Christy's work with college students. These initial meetings formed the basis for a lifetime of co-laboring in ministry in other settings.

Christy made similar visits to many other colleges, including Wellesley, Yale, and Cornell. He arrived at each campus equipped with the names of students with a potential interest in missions. After contacting them, he would encourage them to pray and study the Bible together. And Christy was thrilled to find that this strategy actually worked; college students throughout the Northeast were awakening to the responsibility and privilege of world evangelization.

While the war was winding down, Christy continually prayed and felt a growing burden for missions. He felt compelled to document on paper, just between himself and the Lord, what he believed about the importance of world evangelization, the reality of hell, and the personality of Satan. Most of the tenets he transcribed were ridiculed in the secular world, but they were tenaciously trusted by Christy.

In 1944, Christy attended a Student Volunteer Movement (SVM) convention in Wooster, Ohio. For more than half a century, SVM had played a major role in recruiting students for missionary service throughout the world. However, the organization had been slowly dying since its 1920 quadrennial in Des Moines, Iowa, and by 1944 it had almost completely lost its spiritual missionary emphasis. While at the convention, Christy was in a prayer meeting when one of the SVM leaders came in and broke it up. "We don't want anything emotional going on," he said, admonishing them not to pray.

John R. Mott's address at the convention left a lasting imprint on young Christy. Mott, by then nearly eighty years old, would receive the Nobel Peace Prize two years later, and he had long been one of the greatest missions mobilizers in history. However, Christy could see that his heart was broken by the lack of spiritual vitality in the movement in which he had invested so much of his heart and passion.

Mott shared his spiritual journey with the SVM students. He transported his audience back six decades to when, as a twenty-year-old, he thought his life's work would be either law or his father's lumber business. All of that changed on January 14, 1886, when he walked in late to a lecture being given by J. K. Studd at Cornell. Three sentences in Studd's speech, Mott said, prompted his lifelong service of presenting Christ to students: "Seekest thou great things for thyself? Seek them not. Seek ye first the Kingdom of God." Mott gathered up the courage to meet with the speaker the following day, and he later said that the meeting with Studd was the "decisive hour of his life." Shortly after that he participated in the first SVM convention ever held, led by D. L. Moody. Robert Wilder got ahold of Mott, and a short time later Mott signed a volunteer pledge for missions.

Mott concluded his talk by saying, "Young people, to find Jesus Christ as your Savior and Lord is the most important thing you can do."

After listening to Mott share his story and watching as his heart was breaking, seeds for a new missions conference germinated within Christy's mind. Actually, it would not be new, but rather a continuation of what Moody and Mott had birthed fifty-eight years earlier. Unlike the recent SVM conventions, however, this one would possess a renewed spiritual vitality and missions emphasis.

Christy traveled to the library at McCormick Seminary in Chicago to study the records from the SVM quadrennial conventions of decades past. He studied the speeches that were given, the many topics that were addressed, and the various parts of the world that were highlighted. Through his research, he quickly discovered the path of SVM's demise. It seemed that when you no longer believe in the Bible, you no longer believe in missions. Out of this spiritual void, the Student Foreign Missions Fellowship (SFMF) had been birthed in 1936 to restore the missionary vision abandoned by SVM. SVM would eventually vote itself out of existence.

Christy longed to share with Stacey Woods his vision for launching a missions conference that would bridge the Student Volunteer Movement and InterVarsity. At one point in 1944, when Stacey was planning to visit the Princeton campus, his schedule was completely filled with people desiring to speak with him, so Christy bought a round-trip ticket to the next station where Stacey was traveling and finally got the chance to talk with him. "Stacey, I'm really burdened for missions," Christy implored, "because the war is winding down, and I think this is going to be the great opportunity to challenge young people with completing Christ's commission. And I'm very concerned that InterVarsity be more involved in this."

Stacey listened intently. "Fine, Christy, you go and organize it," he finally replied.

The next thing Christy knew, Stacey was informing him that the IVCF board had voted him missionary secretary of IVCF for the United States and Canada.

Princeton had a special policy at that time for students with an A average: as long as they spent their time in research or other pursuits, they did not have to attend lectures but simply had to take the exams. This allowed Christy to spend much of his time at the University of Chicago, where he lived at the international house, leading international students to Christ and starting Bible studies.

When Christy finally returned to Princeton, the president of the seminary, Dr. John Alexander Mackay, confronted him about his faraway endeavors. "You know, we didn't set this up so that students could leave campus. It's just so that students can do research," Dr. Mackay complained.

"Well, Dr. Mackay," Christy retorted, "you were a missionary in Latin America, and you know how important it is to help students in relation to missions."

"Quite so, quite so," the president replied, and nothing more was ever said about it. Christy continued to travel extensively and work full-time with IVCF during his time in seminary.

In 1945, SFMF merged with IVCF, forming the missionary arm of InterVarsity. IVCF was working on secular campuses, while SFMF had chapters on Christian college campuses. With the merger, plans for the first IVCF student missions conference began to accelerate.

Shortly after graduating from Princeton Seminary in December of that year, Christy assumed his new role as missionary secretary, as well as that of associate general secretary. He continued to travel to college campuses, but his responsibility now grew from New England and New York to all of the United States and Canada.

During one cross-country venture he traveled west to British Columbia, then south along the West Coast into California.

By the time he reached California, he was totally out of money, unable even to buy his next train ticket. However, a woman to whom he had been witnessing during one of the rides gave him twenty dollars, allowing him to venture on.

Christy headed east to Dallas Theological Seminary in Texas and then north to Chicago, visiting universities, Christian colleges, and Bible schools along the way and inviting students everywhere to the upcoming missions conference. When he arrived in Chicago, he had to fast for several days because he was once again totally out of money. One of the students on the campus had a chocolate bar and gave Christy half of it, and that was all Christy had to eat the entire weekend.

During his travels in January 1946, Christy heard Billy Graham for the first time. Graham, then just twenty-seven years old, was a staff member with Youth for Christ and was relatively unknown. Christy long remembered being impressed with the young evangelist.

On February 24, shortly after starting his next cross-country adventure, Christy wrote to his parents:

> Well the trip has started and I am now in Minneapolis. Last night I met with some students at the University of Minnesota, tonight I speak to the young people at the First Baptist Church and then tomorrow at the Northwestern School of Theology and Bible School. Thank you so much for all your prayers, because in myself I feel miserably inadequate.

While traveling in western Canada in March, he visited Prairie Bible Institute in Alberta. He later told the story of a life-changing night during that trip:

> There I told students how this was the greatest opportunity in history to evangelize the world. The

war was over, China was open, and other countries were now accessible.

"Before the Lord chose His disciples, He prayed all night," I told them. "Where are these all-night prayer meetings now?"

But even as I spoke, the Holy Spirit convicted me of being a hypocrite since I had never spent a night in prayer. And here I was preaching beyond my depth.

Consequently, I decided to pray all night. Now, it's one thing to decide to spend the night in prayer, but it's another thing to know what to pray for during that time.

I had just finished reading a book by Robert Wilder, whom God used to start the Student Volunteer Movement. In this he had noted that the Bible study that meant the most to him was examining the Person and work of the Holy Spirit in Scripture. So I decided that I would take my concordance and study the Person and work of the Holy Spirit for half-an-hour from the Bible, and then pray for half-an-hour, and continue doing this throughout the night.

Towards morning, while I was praying and asking the Lord what He wanted me to do, I sensed the Lord speaking to me. I didn't hear an audible voice, but the Lord impressed this thought on my mind.

"Are you willing to do anything for me?"

"Yes, Lord," I answered. "I'm willing to do anything for You."

Then the Lord's voice came once more.

"Are you willing to die for Me?"

"Lord," I whispered, "You died for me, so I'll gladly die for Thee." And as I prayed that, something totally unexpected happened. The Holy Spirit fell on me in power. Completely and unexpectedly the power of God came upon me in waves as I was baptized in the Holy Spirit. His love, joy, peace, and other fruit was multiplied in my life.

The next morning when I spoke in chapel, the Lord worked in a new way. Many students volunteered for missions.

While serving as missionary secretary, Christy led the planning of the new IVCF missions conference. Stacey Woods, Will Norton, and Mary Ann Klein labored alongside Christy throughout the planning process. Will Norton was on his first furlough from missionary service in Africa. Since he had been active with SFMF, he was a great help in the merger and the cooperative venture of the missions conference. He later described Christy's passion as "a zeal bordering on desperation."

During the summer of 1946, the planning team gathered for a staff conference with much brainstorming regarding the upcoming missions conference. They were heavily dependent on the InterVarsity staff scattered across the United States and Canada for recruiting students.

The planning team selected the University of Toronto as the site of their first conference, noting that InterVarsity had been in Canada longer than in the United States. Desiring to establish a bridge between the new IVCF missions conference in Toronto and the great SVM missions conventions of decades past, Christy and his team invited Samuel Zwemer and Harold Ockenga, both longtime leaders of the SVM, to be keynote speakers. The theme of the Toronto conference was "Complete Christ's Commission."

Christy and his team planned the conference with several objectives and hopes. First, at a time when there were twice as many women as men on the mission field, they sought to encourage men to become missionaries. They carefully accepted equal numbers of men and women as attendees at the conference. Second, they sought to challenge the participants with the evangelization of the world. With the war ending, it seemed that every mission field was opening—Russia was open, China was open, and Communism had not yet taken hold in distant regions of the world. A third objective was to lay hold of God in prayer. Stacey Woods later observed that he had never seen a conference covered in so much prayer as this one.

Finally, on Friday, December 27, just two days after Christmas, the first IVCF missions conference began. Approximately fifty-two denominations were represented by 576 students from 151 colleges, universities, and seminaries. The slate of speakers assembled by Christy and his team was impressive: Robert McQuilkin from Columbia Bible College, whose talk at Wheaton in 1936 helped spark the formation of SFMF; Calvin Chao, leader of the China Native Evangelism Crusade; Gordon Holdcroft of the Independent Board of Presbyterian Missions; Leslie Maxwell, founder of the Three Hills Bible Institute in Alberta; Bakht Singh, an influential missionary leader on the Indian subcontinent; and Dr. Zwemer and Dr. Ockenga.

Christy also invited the president of the university to briefly greet and welcome the assembly. Since the president was going to be out of town, he asked a colleague, J. Burgon Bickersteth, to extend a greeting to the conference participants. However, Bickersteth's words were anything but welcoming—instead, he seized the opportunity to lambast the group. "Why are you hiding out? Why can't you get along with other Christians? Why do you have to start InterVarsity?" The assembled students sat in stunned disbelief at such an unexpected attack.

The next speaker, Dr. Ockenga, calmly walked to the speaker's podium. "Since you asked, Mr. Bickersteth, these are the reasons why we are here and what we are doing," he began. He then proceeded to answer each of Bickersteth's questions, one by one, carefully and thoughtfully. Finally, he launched into his prepared message.

The atmosphere in the assembly hall was electric, and the conference was launched with a rousing start.

Long after the conference concluded on January 2, Stacey Woods observed that over half of the participants had actually gone to the foreign mission field, with the other half actively supporting missions from home. Among the participants in that first conference were Jim Elliot, martyred seeking to bring the gospel to the Waodani people of Ecuador nine years later; David Howard, who became a missionary to Colombia and president of Latin America Mission; and Ralph Winter, the great missionary strategist for the unreached peoples of the world.

The missions conference continued through future decades, but with a few changes: it was relocated to the more central location of Urbana, Illinois (and most recently to St. Louis, Missouri, though it is still called Urbana), and changed from every two years to every three to allow more time for planning. The triennial Urbana missions conference continues to this day. It has grown to become the largest student missions conference in the world, and through it God has challenged more than 250,000 participants with the responsibility and privilege of taking part in world missions.

Throughout Christy's four years on staff with InterVarsity, his passion to find a way into Afghanistan never diminished or wavered. He was simply waiting on the Lord while mobilizing students to evangelize other distant reaches of the world. Little did Christy realize that, soon after the conference, the way into Afghanistan would open for self-supporting Christian workers. Eleven participants in that first conference would end up in Afghanistan.

Neither did he realize that, before the conference ended, he would lay eyes on his future bride for the first time.

CHAPTER 5
BETTY

"At last!" the man exclaimed. "This one is bone from my bone, and flesh from my flesh! She will be called 'woman,' because she was taken from 'man.'" This explains why a man leaves his father and mother and is joined to his wife, and the two are united into one.
Genesis 2:23–24

On the day Christy and Betty first met, he may have known that she would one day become his wife. But he could not have known that, three and a half years later on their honeymoon, an irate lodge keeper would chase them through the upstairs hallway—due to a simple misunderstanding—until they had darted into the safety of their locked room.

On December 28, 1946, Christy's mind was fully engaged with his responsibilities of directing the first InterVarsity missions conference, which was then into its second day. Among the 576 students at the University of Toronto for the conference was Betty Jean Hutton, a twenty-two-year-old brown-eyed, auburn-haired kindergarten teacher from Hamilton, Ontario.

Betty didn't really want to be there. She had been hoping to spend Christmas with her grandmother in Ottawa. She was also nervous about participating in a missions conference, not knowing what she might be getting herself into. But since she had been selected as a delegate of the Teachers Christian Fellowship, a branch of IVCF, she gave in and decided to go.

Many of Betty's friends had recently gotten married, and she was a bridesmaid in their weddings. Feeling particularly discouraged one day, Betty knelt by her bed at home and prayed, "Lord, you know I don't know anybody, and if you want me to get married, you'll have to bring that person who you want for me. If you don't want me to be married and you want me to be single, that's alright too." Betty put her love life squarely in the Lord's hands. The next thing she knew, she was at the missions conference.

On the first day, the participants were welcomed to Toronto by a vicious ice storm that slammed the city and made transportation treacherous. One of the first speakers, Bakht Singh, had just arrived from the heat of India, and he promptly slipped on an icy sidewalk, breaking his right arm in numerous places. The doctors warned him that they would need to open up his whole arm to reset the bones. Mr. Singh informed them that any such surgery would simply have to wait until after he had addressed the assembled students. So with his Bible in his left hand and his right arm in a sling, he delivered an impassioned message on "counting the cost." He challenged the assembled students, "Young people, don't follow Christ lightly. He gave his life for the world; he wants you to give your life. Be willing to pay the cost."

Bakht Singh's message spoke to Betty's heart, and she sensed that God was calling her to go somewhere as a missionary. A simple, heartfelt prayer rose within her: "Lord, I'll go; please show me where."

Samuel Zwemer also addressed the auditorium full of students. Dr. Zwemer was the first long-term American missionary to the Middle East, founded and edited the quarterly publication *The Moslem World* for thirty-seven years, and directly motivated hundreds of workers for foreign missions during his life. One of them was Betty Hutton. When Zwemer suggested to the students, "Some of the best people to work among Muslims are kindergarten teachers," Betty's heart jumped. She felt as though Zwemer were speaking to her alone.

When he finished his address, Betty yearned to speak with him personally. She longed to learn more about how God might use a kindergarten teacher from Hamilton, Ontario, to grow his kingdom in this big world. But how could she ever find a way to meet him?

Someone suggested to her that she speak with an IVCF staff member named Christy Wilson. "Christy will help you speak with Dr. Zwemer," they assured her. So Betty sought out Christy Wilson. And she found him.

Shortly after their introduction and initial conversation, Christy and Betty both had strong reactions—but very different ones. Christy knew that he had just met the woman he would one day marry: "It was love at first sight. I had told the Lord I would be willing to be single all my life if that were his will, and she had also told the Lord that she'd be willing to be single. But I knew right then that she was the one that God had chosen for me."

And Betty's reaction? Initially, she had no inkling that this young man was interested in her at all. (They would have no further conversations at the conference, and it would be more than a year before Christy revealed his feelings to her.) In addition, she had second thoughts about talking with Dr. Zwemer. Instead she decided to visit the United Church of Canada booth, which represented the church in which she had been raised. The prayer that accompanied her throughout the remainder of the conference was, "Lord, if being a missionary through the United Church of Canada isn't what you want for me, please close that door."

During Christy's next trip home following the missions conference, he cautiously queried his mother, "What color hair should my wife have?"

Not yet knowing anything about his encounter with Betty, her motherly response was, "It doesn't really matter—any color is fine—just as long as you get a wife."

But Christy persisted, "What about a redhead?"

"No, no," she insisted, "never marry a redhead!"

Betty was clearly a redhead. She was also the only girl Christy had ever really looked at and wanted to date. Meanwhile the Spirit of God was planting within Betty's heart that quality Christy most sought in a wife: a willingness and desire to go to the mission field.

When Betty returned home from the conference, she was thrilled about what God had spoken to her heart. As secretary in her local Teachers Christian Fellowship chapter, one of her first responsibilities was to correspond with Christy to invite him to come and speak to their group. Christy accepted the invitation and came to Hamilton. Though his visit was brief, they both enjoyed being together again. During a follow-up trip to Hamilton, Christy called Betty and asked if she would join him for dinner. Again they had a lovely time together. Shortly after that, he asked if she would travel to Toronto to see the concert of the *St. Matthew Passion* with him. She gladly accepted and traveled by train to meet him for their concert date in Toronto. Following the concert, Christy saw her back to the train. During a third trip to Hamilton for a speaking engagement, Christy again contacted Betty and took her out to dinner.

Christy and Betty had shared three dates together. Then one day he called while she was away at Canadian Girls in Training as a camp leader. He had called to tell her goodbye—he was about to venture off to Scotland to begin his doctoral studies at the University of Edinburgh.

It was late summer of 1947 when Christy departed, and he would not return until the summer of 1949. They were to be apart for two very long years.

When he left, Betty had already begun to be interested in him. She felt at home with him from the start, and she was thrilled that he had visited her in Hamilton and had wanted to take her out. But they had shared only a few dates together, and because he so energetically encouraged people in missions, she couldn't help wondering, *Is he really interested in me, or is he merely interested in the fact that I might want to be a missionary? Could he really be interested in someone like me?* Betty was afraid to get her hopes up.

During his studies in Edinburgh they corresponded about once a month, and he wrote quite openly about his life in Scotland. Betty answered each letter. Christy wrote about the people he had met and described his studies. They were wonderful letters, but they were also the kind Betty could share with her mother without the slightest embarrassment.

But one day a letter arrived in which he had enclosed a picture of himself. He asked her for one of herself in return.

Photos exchanged by Christy and Betty at the start of their courtship
Courtesy of the Wilson family

Then as February 14 approached, a Valentine's Day card arrived from him signed "Affectionately, Christy." It was her first inkling of any love interest on his part.

Their correspondence continued throughout his doctoral studies in Scotland. Shortly before he was to return to the United States, a letter arrived from Christy that excited Betty once again. He quoted to her 2 John 1:12 (using the King James Version, the only translation widely available at that time): "Having many things to write unto you, I would not write with paper and ink: but I trust to come unto you, and speak face to face, that our joy may be full." And he did. Shortly after earning his PhD in Islamic studies, he returned to Canada and quickly made his way to Hamilton. He was on a single-minded quest with a question for a certain Canadian kindergarten teacher.

Dressed in a blue pinstripe seersucker suit, he looked very attractive, at least in Betty's eyes—the only eyes that really mattered on that day. Betty's mother cooked a lamb dinner for the four of them, and at the end of the meal, Christy suggested, "Betty, how about if we go for a walk?"

Since Hamilton is located along the Niagara Escarpment, it is rich in natural beauty. As Christy escorted Betty on a walk in the woods behind her house, he asked her if she would be his wife. Betty inadvertently hesitated, and Christy offered, "Do you want to think about it?" But she quickly made it clear that she wanted to marry him.

When they arrived back at Betty's home following their trek in the woods, they told her mother and father the news. Mr. Hutton knew that Christy had his eyes set on Afghanistan, and the prospect of Christy taking his daughter to such a distant, unfamiliar land concerned him. But he also loved Christy, so the parents were very pleased with the announcement.

Christy didn't yet have a ring to offer Betty, but he spent that whole summer pastoring at a church in Princeton until he could afford a proper engagement ring for his fiancée.

Meanwhile Betty worked at the InterVarsity Pioneer Camp, and she was surprised when Christy's younger sister, Nancy, suddenly appeared with plans to be a camp counselor also. They got acquainted and had a delightful summer together.

Near the end of her time at camp, Christy unexpectedly appeared and again suggested, "Let's go for a walk." Some of Betty's fellow campers followed them, and it was there that Christy gave her a beautiful engagement ring.

In the fall of 1949, Christy enrolled at Columbia University, and he arranged for Betty to study at Biblical Seminary, which was also in New York City. Betty took courses in Bible and children's education, while Christy took a course in teaching English as a second language (TESL), hoping that it might provide an entrée into Afghanistan. He also pastored a small church in Palisades, just north of New York City.

Christy continued to live in Princeton that fall, while Betty lived in New York City. She was there for just a year, but it was a wonderful year. Her mind soaked in the teaching like a parched sponge, and they were able to be together after having been separated for so long. With their eyes set on Afghanistan, they began to prepare themselves. They went to all kinds of ethnic restaurants, acquainting themselves with various international foods. They also took a medical course for non-medical missionaries, which proved to be a most frightening experience for both of them. They were required to interact with large worms that can get into people's systems. Christy would later reflect that taking that course was one of the worst things he had ever done.

Finally their wedding day arrived. On June 14, 1950, Christy and Betty were married in her home church in Hamilton, the Melrose United Church of Canada. About seventy-five relatives and friends were congregated in its sanctuary, modeled after the Gothic-style Melrose Abbey in Scotland. Betty's pastor, John Mutch, a man who was deeply respected by the Hutton family, performed the ceremony, and Christy Sr. also took part in it.

Since the school at which Betty taught kindergarten was near the church, most of her students gathered in the narthex. They were excited to be at their teacher's wedding and expressed their excitement with much rambunctiousness and noise. In the middle of the ceremony, Dr. Mutch paused and requested, "Could someone please take those children outside?"

After signing the registry, Christy and Betty Wilson walked down the aisle as husband and wife.

They were planning to depart for their honeymoon by train, but the master of

Betty and Christy on their wedding day
Courtesy of the Wilson family

ceremonies, an InterVarsity man, graciously offered them the use of his car. (He also surprised everyone at the wedding by announcing his own engagement.) Christy and Betty drove up to the Muskoka area, a summer resort north of Toronto. They stayed at the Big Chief Lodge and visited several nearby places. On Sunday morning, they went to the Salvation Army church near the Lake of Bays. An InterVarsity camp known as Campus in the Woods was located at the head of the lake.

"Wouldn't it be fun," Christy suggested, "to rent a canoe and go over and visit the campers?" Having come right from church, Betty was not dressed for such an adventure, still wearing her high-heel shoes and a camel-hair coat. Nevertheless, they climbed into the canoe and set off for the other side of the lake. When they arrived, they were warmly welcomed by the IVCF leaders who were meeting there that week, and the afternoon flew by.

On their way back across the lake, a wind suddenly came upon them and flipped their canoe right over. It was to be the only time Betty would ever see Christy look truly afraid. "Hang on to the canoe," he implored her, "hang on to the canoe!"

Since the people at the IVCF campsite had let them get away without taking a photograph, they pursued the newlyweds in their motorboat, only to find them hanging on to their canoe for dear life. By the time they rescued the drenched couple and got them to shore, Betty's dress had shrunk almost all the way up to her neck— or so it seemed to her.

They were startled to find, tucked away in their soggy clothes, all the checks that people had so kindly given to them as wedding gifts. Since the checks were now soaked in lake water and therefore useless, they later had to humbly write to each person asking if they would mind rewriting their check.

When they finally got back to the lodge, they were both eager to return to some semblance of warmth and privacy. Not wanting anyone in the hotel lobby to see them in their present state of disarray, they climbed up the fire escape to the second floor, made their way into the building, and dashed down the hall.

The manager of the Big Chief Lodge, seeing these two disheveled creatures climbing up the fire escape of his hotel, set off in pursuit of the trespassers. Christy and Betty hastened down the hallway, made a quick turn, and retreated into the safety of their locked room before the manager could catch them. They later tracked him down, told him the whole by-that-time-hilarious story, and apologized for the trouble they had caused.

So began married life for Christy and Betty Wilson. Together they were to share many more adventures, many more encounters with those in authority, and many more close calls. But they were also to share forty-eight years as partners in life, ministry, parenthood, and love. It would still be another year before they finally set foot on Afghan soil—a year filled with many twists and turns, but nevertheless one marked by God's guiding hand and his abundant goodness.

CHAPTER 6
A ROUNDABOUT
ROUTE TO
AFGHANISTAN

*"Therefore, go and make disciples of all the nations, baptizing them
in the name of the Father and the Son and the Holy Spirit. Teach these
new disciples to obey all the commands I have given you. And be
sure of this: I am with you always, even to the end of the age."*
Matthew 28:19–20

It was early afternoon on Friday, June 22, 1951, and Christy's heart
was beating with anticipation. He was scheduled to depart for Afghanistan in just three days, having been waiting four long years
for this day to arrive. He was prepared to fly from New York, and
nothing could keep him off that plane.

Except the fact that one essential item was missing—his
passport.

Surely it must have been mailed to the wrong address, he reasoned,
not wanting to imagine any more obstacles. He went directly to the
United States Passport Division office to test his theory.

He was sent from one office to another. Eventually he found
himself standing in front of a large desk belonging to the director
of the Passport Division. After a series of questions and objections
from the director, the truth began to settle on Christy: His passport
had *not* been lost in the mail. In fact, the State Department had no
intention of issuing one.

As he stood there waiting, his mind raced back to the previous
times he had come so close to departing for Afghanistan only to
experience a last-minute setback.

His first letdown had come four years earlier. It was February 1947 when he first learned of a need for teachers in Afghanistan. Shortly after the first InterVarsity missions conference, a student noticed a posting on the bulletin board at Columbia Teachers College in New York stating that teachers were wanted in Afghanistan. Living and ministering in Afghanistan had been his heart's passion since he was a child, and the opportunity was now staring him straight in the face.

Some of Christy's closest friends tried to dissuade him. "It would be foolhardy to go to a closed country where there is no freedom to proclaim the gospel," they reasoned. "You should go to a free country where you can witness without restraints. Then when Afghanistan finally becomes open, you can go there to evangelize." Christy confessed that he did not know what God had in store; he knew only that the Holy Spirit had told him to go.

Along with several other Christians, Christy completed the necessary paperwork and submitted his application. Anticipating that he would soon be departing for Afghanistan, he notified InterVarsity that he would be resigning from his position as missionary secretary that summer. However, as the months passed, Christy heard nothing in response to his application, so he made temporary alternate plans to go to Edinburgh, where he would continue his education and better prepare himself for ministry in a Muslim nation.

The very day he boarded the *Queen Elizabeth* to sail for Scotland, a letter arrived at his home asking him to come to Washington, DC, for an interview. The letter was forwarded to Christy in Scotland, and he promptly replied, "I am now working on a doctorate but would be more than willing to interrupt my studies if you want me to go to Afghanistan."

The reply stated, "There is no need for you to return to the States for an interview. We have had enough applications. Continue your studies and reapply after you have earned your degree."

Christy was disappointed. However, that first delay allowed him to write his dissertation, which focused on Muhammad's prophetic office as portrayed in the Quran, and the knowledge he gained during his two years in Edinburgh proved valuable during the decades he would spend ministering in Afghanistan.

Yet another setback struck Christy several years later. In the summer of 1949, shortly after returning to the US from Scotland, he met with Dick Soderberg, who was recruiting faculty for the new Afghan Institute of Technology (AIT). "Would you be willing to head up AIT's English Department?" Dick asked. Christy readily agreed. During his months of waiting, he took courses at Columbia in linguistics and teaching English as a second language.

When Christy and Betty were married in June 1950, they fully expected to be departing for Afghanistan any day. They didn't even bother to unpack their wedding gifts since everything would soon need to be packed once again anyway. However, as time passed with no word from their prospective employer, they grew more and more uneasy.

Then, in the fall of 1950, a letter arrived from Dick with unwelcome news. An American family living in Afghanistan knew that Christy's parents had been missionaries in Iran, and they assumed that he was coming to Afghanistan for the same purpose. As this rumor spread, the staff at AIT decided that Christy wasn't worth the risk. Allowing a missionary to enter Afghanistan was, of course, unacceptable to the Muslim authorities, and bringing him on board could endanger the fledgling school. "You'd better wait for three to five more years until the matter is forgotten," Dick advised.

Once again, Christy and Betty found their plans thwarted. Nearly four years had passed since Christy had first applied to teach in Afghanistan. But God encouraged them with a promise from Numbers 14:8: "If the LORD is pleased with us, then he will bring us into this land, and give it to us." They pressed on with the assurance that God was faithful and trustworthy; if they obediently followed his lead, he would surely open the way for them.

Shortly after their wedding, Christy's mother offered him some unsolicited counsel. "Christy," she admonished, "when Betty says, 'I'm hungry,' what are you going to do? It's great to plan on going to Afghanistan, but now you have a wife! You have to feed her, so you need to get a job." So Christy applied for pastoral work while they waited.

One church in Pennsylvania asked him to sign a contract for two years. "I'm sorry," Christy replied. "I've applied to go to Afghanistan. I want to be free to go whenever the door opens."

"If that's the case," they replied, "we can't accept you."

Before long, Herbert Mekeel, pastor of the First Presbyterian Church in Schenectady, invited Christy to help plant a daughter church in nearby East Glenville. Christy told Mekeel the same thing he had told the other church. "Wonderful!" Mekeel replied. "Whenever God opens the door for you to go to Afghanistan, that's when we want you to go! Come for a few weeks, a few months, a few years, or whatever it is. Then when the door to Afghanistan opens for you, you'll have praying people behind you."

Once again, this new delay proved to be profitable in preparing them for their future work in Afghanistan. As they waited, they grew in pastoral experience that would be invaluable when they finally arrived in Kabul and became connected with many praying people who stood behind their vision. Christy served the church in East Glenville for only eight months, but the church kept him as their minister *extra muros*, or minister "outside the walls," for over forty years.

During those eight months of ministry in New York, Christy and Betty had very little money. Their first home consisted of a bedroom, a kitchen, and a small living room, and they had to stand sideways to squeeze into their bathroom. For transportation, someone loaned Christy a car, complete with everything except a muffler. Betty said she could hear her new husband a mile away when he was on his way home.

Nevertheless, the young couple was filled with joy, basking in their new marriage, thriving in their first pastoral assignment together, and eagerly awaiting the day they could go to Afghanistan. And even as previous doors had been closed for Christy and

Betty, God was already at work answering their prayers and opening another.

In early 1951, Frank Laubach, often referred to as the "apostle to the illiterates," was putting the finishing touches on a literacy project in Afghanistan. A United Nations survey taken at that time had revealed that 97 percent of the Afghan people could not read or write. To help remedy this problem, the Afghan Ministry of Education had invited Dr. Laubach to develop reading curricula for the Dari and Pushtu languages. Dr. Laubach and his literacy team accepted the challenge and completed their work in March.

At the farewell reception for the literacy team, Abdul Majid, minister of education, informed Dr. Laubach that he was in need of a man with very specific qualifications—so specific that he feared such a person could not be found. He was seeking someone with a PhD who had training in the most current methods of teaching English and who also knew the languages of the Muslim world.

Dr. Laubach knew just the person—J. Christy Wilson Jr. He encouraged Majid to speak with Christy's father, who had served on the literacy team as an interpreter. Christy Sr. promptly provided Majid with his son's address.

Shortly after that, Christy received a cable from the Ministry of Education offering him an English-teaching position at Habibia High School in Kabul, the oldest secondary school in the country and one of Afghanistan's most respected institutions for high school boys. This sudden change in circumstances was almost unbelievable. Christy later reflected, "Betty and I were overwhelmed by the ways of God. After four years of red tape and frustration, my hands held a personal invitation from the top Afghan education official."

With this door of opportunity flung wide open, Christy traveled to Washington, DC, to speak with the acting Afghan ambassador. Before signing the contract to teach at Habibia, he felt it only right to inform the ambassador that he was a Christian minister. He didn't want anyone—the ambassador or any other officials—to ever feel that he had entered Afghanistan under false pretenses.

The ambassador assured Christy that this was not a problem. "Most Afghan teachers are Muslim *mullahs*, clerics," he told Christy. "It will be good to have a Christian minister teaching our young people."

Christy also sought to clarify a troublesome clause in his contract that required him "not to interfere in business, politics, and/or religion." Christy asked exactly what this meant. "If a student asks me a religious question, does this mean that I am not free to answer him?"

"By no means," the ambassador replied. "If a student asks you a question, then as a teacher, you have an obligation to answer." Grateful for this clarification, Christy promptly signed the contract. His father, who had accompanied him to Washington, DC, served as a witness and carefully documented the conversation for future reference:

> Before you leave for Afghanistan, I think it might be well for me to set down some of the points of our recent conversation with the officials of the Afghan Embassy in Washington. . . .
>
> We brought up the matter of the clause in your contract stating that you would not interfere with the religion or the politics of Afghanistan while you were there under the contract. We stated that you would use the utmost tact and did not intend to speak against Islam or to meddle in politics in any way, and it was our understanding that this was the meaning of the clause. On the other hand we were assured by the Embassy officials that it was not intended to limit personal freedom of speech or statement of one's personal beliefs in a tactful and sympathetic way to make certain that there would be no interference with the state religion or criticism of it as such and *no* political activity.

All seemed to be progressing smoothly—until four days before his scheduled flight. Christy received a phone call from the Afghan embassy. "We are not sure you are going after all!" the secretary's voice on the other end informed him.

"Can you tell me the reason?" Christy asked. "My contract has already been signed and authorized." The secretary replied that he could not discuss it over the telephone; Christy would have to come and meet with the ambassador again in person.

Christy and Betty called friends throughout the country that night, urging them to pray for his trip to Washington. Their prayers surrounded him the next day as he met with the Afghan ambassador.

The ambassador said that he wanted to ensure that Christy understood the religious conditions in Afghanistan. "Since I grew up in Iran," Christy responded, "I am quite familiar with Muslim people. My desire is to help the Afghan nation and people, and I have no intention of causing any trouble."

The ambassador, convinced of Christy's integrity, conveyed his appreciation that Christy was going to work among his people. As he served Christy tea, he paused and asked, "Would you mind doing me a favor?" He walked out of the room and returned with half a dozen new Arrow shirts. "Would you mind delivering these to the prime minister in Kabul?" Christy assured him that he would do so.

However, he still hadn't received his passport, and shortly after exchanging farewells with the ambassador, he found himself standing in the plush office of Ms. Shipley, director of the US Passport Division. Although he had been cleared by the Afghan government, he still faced a series of questions from representatives of his own country.

"What is your primary purpose for going to Afghanistan?" the director asked pointedly. "Do you intend to preach the gospel?"

"I know Afghanistan does not have religious freedom," Christy answered, as honestly as he knew how, "but I believe God is going to open that land. When he does, I will count it a privilege to tell the people about my Lord."

"That's what we were afraid of!" the director erupted, pounding her fist on the desk. "By the way, what has the Afghan embassy said about your going?"

"I've just come from tea with the ambassador in his office," Christy replied, describing their recent conversation.

Ms. Shipley was rapidly running out of options. US law stated that international travel privileges could only be denied to those seeking the forcible overthrow of the American government, and such was clearly not the case for the pastor standing before her. She knew she had no legal grounds to deny Christy's passport application. In one final effort to dissuade him, she sent him from office to office, and each official he encountered delivered the same impassioned plea: He simply must not go. It would be madness for a pastor to move to a land as rigidly Islamic as Afghanistan. Not only was the country resistant to Christian influence, but it would be dangerous for the Wilsons.

Betty and Christy leaving for Afghanistan in 1951
Courtesy of the Wilson family

But God had called Christy to serve him in Afghanistan, and he had seen God's providential hand guide him this far. He was not about to let any Washington bureaucrats deter him. Just before closing for the weekend, the State Department reluctantly approved Christy's passport. As a result, Christy and Betty were able to board a flight bound for Peshawar, Pakistan, the following Monday.

• • •

When Christy and Betty arrived in Peshawar two weeks later, the thermostat at the Dean's Hotel registered 115 degrees. Christy wrote his initial observations upon arriving in Pakistan:

> It is quite a shock to be parachuted into these surroundings with the poverty, smells and strange

food. But the Lord has given us a real love for these people. How they respond to a smile and a little interest in their problems! The opportunities for service here are overwhelming, both spiritually and materially. May the Lord of the harvest call many more laborers to come and serve Him here.

Christy and Betty didn't know how they would travel the final 180 miles from Peshawar to Kabul. Since Afghanistan had no plane service at that time, it required an overland journey through the Khyber Pass, and the only public passenger transportation was a truck that had been adapted into a bus with hard wooden seats. Since Betty was now five months pregnant, Christy decided that a ride in the back of a converted truck over rough mountain roads was not an option. On the other hand, neither could they afford the two-hundred-dollar fare for a trip that taxis only made infrequently.

Christy and Betty did what they had done so many times before: they committed the matter to the Lord in prayer and then watched him provide for their needs yet again.

That evening they were forcing down a greasy curry dinner in the hotel dining room when a British gentleman approached their table and addressed them: "Dr. and Mrs. Wilson, I want to welcome you to Afghanistan. I just want you to know there's a brand new Chevrolet station wagon with a chauffeur ready to drive you to Kabul tomorrow morning." Then he was gone. Christy and Betty sat together in stunned silence.

After they finished dinner, Christy sought out the hotel manager. "Excuse me, sir, who was that man who came and spoke to me?" he inquired.

"Oh, he's from the United Nations," the manager replied. "He just arrived from Afghanistan with a chauffeur-driven station wagon and asked me if any UN specialists had come in. I pointed you out."

"But I'm not with the United Nations," Christy informed him. He asked for the UN man's room number and went to speak with him.

"Sir," Christy explained, "I so appreciate your coming to our table and offering us the use of a car, because my wife and I are looking for transportation to Kabul. But I must tell you that I'm not with the United Nations."

"Oh, you aren't?" he replied.

"No," Christy said.

"I'll tell you what," he told him. "The car has to go back anyway. You and your wife go and take anyone you want along with you." So Christy and Betty ended up locating the UN specialist for whom Christy had been mistaken and traveling with him and his wife to Kabul.

The Wilsons' plan had been to leave Peshawar early enough to arrive in Kabul at the home of Howard Larsen, Habibia's American principal, the same day. As usual, things did not go according to plan. In the first of many hundreds of letters written on Afghan soil, Christy described their journey to Kabul in a July 12 note to his parents:

> Here we are in Kabul after a glorious trip all the way. . . . We had a most comfortable ride up for nothing, and made the trip easily in one day! The car didn't leave Peshawar until almost 11:00 and therefore with several stops on the way for tea we didn't get into Kabul until around 11:00 that night. It being so late, we didn't want to bother the Larsens and therefore put up in the Hotel de Kabul for the night.

In 1951, Kabul was far from being a metropolitan hub, and the hotel reception desk had already closed by the time they arrived. When the chauffeur knocked on the door, a sleepy-eyed manager eventually emerged and escorted Christy and Betty to a filthy room. The bed sheets were spotted with blood stains where former occupants had killed malaria-spreading mosquitoes.

"We can't stay here," Betty said to Christy. "We must go to another hotel!"

As Christy formulated his reply, his mind returned to their wedding vows a year earlier—*for better or for worse.* "This is the only one there is," he responded apologetically.

Indeed, it was the only hotel in all of Kabul, the capital of a poor country with an agrarian economy. Poverty was evident in the houses and dress of the people, yet their dignity did not allow for begging on the streets. Christy and Betty quickly observed that Afghans were friendly and hospitable to strangers, curious about the outsiders' strange ways but eager to get to know them. The warmth and sense of humor that Kabul's citizens displayed, and the beauty and mystery of this ancient city, drew many visitors to return again and again.

When Christy and Betty first arrived in Afghanistan, there were fifty-two different languages spoken in the country and over one hundred people groups. The number of known Afghan Christians was zero.

CHAPTER 7
A MODERN TENTMAKER AND A CROWN PRINCE

Paul lived and worked with them, for they were tentmakers
just as he was. Each Sabbath found Paul at the synagogue,
trying to convince the Jews and Greeks alike.
Acts 18:3-4

In 1951, no businessman, no explorer, no tourist, and certainly no missionary was allowed in Afghanistan. The country was a no-man's-land with a strict "no trespassing" policy. Due to its geography, it had long served as a buffer zone between the two great powers of Russia and India, and the policy of isolation held by its freedom-loving people prevented external interference and permitted strong adherence to Islam. Although missionaries had worked and prayed all along the Afghan border for many decades, entrance into the country was continually and strictly forbidden.

But now Christy found himself standing on soil where few Christian witnesses had ever stood before.

Just four years earlier the British Empire had pulled out of the Indian subcontinent and Pakistan had separated from India. Now Afghanistan was free to develop its own foreign policy. The government quickly realized that they needed teachers to help their young people catch up with the rest of the world. In this political climate, the Afghan government gladly granted Christy a visa, covered his travel expenses, and paid him a small salary to teach English in Kabul.

Shortly after the Wilsons' arrival, an Afghan diplomat who had been serving in the Washington embassy filled in some of the missing pieces regarding the opposition Christy had encountered at the US State Department. "When you applied for your passport," the diplomat explained, "a CIA security check was run on you, and they found out that you are an ordained minister. The State Department therefore advised the Afghan embassy to cancel your contract, stating that you would be a dangerous person to have in this area." The diplomat then added, displaying the independent Afghan spirit, "But we did not listen to the State Department!"

The suspicion did not end after Christy arrived in Afghanistan. During his first month in Kabul, Christy wrote a letter to his parents with the following coded caution:

> One thing you might pray about is that we know on good authority that the U.S. Embassy here is investigating us as ἀπόστολοι [apostoloi; Greek for "apostles," "messengers," or "ones sent on a mission"]. For this reason, it might be best not to use Sem. [Seminary] stationery. Also our mail coming to the above place could easily be read by them. If anything comes of this, I shall let you know as soon as possible since you might have to go to bat for us in Washington.

Furthermore, Christy soon learned that the Afghan government was very distrustful of foreigners, suspecting that they might have hidden motives. They assigned two secret police to every foreigner permitted into the country—one to keep watch during the day and the other at night. From the time Christy first set foot on Afghan soil, government workers were watching his every move.

The Kabul that Christy and Betty first encountered was quite small: someone could practically drive through the city without even realizing they were there. The city's central area had several shops but no high-rise buildings. A blue mosque dominated the downtown section, located along the edge of Kabul's only paved road. Perched a mile high in the snow-capped mountains of the

Hindu Kush, Kabul experienced the variety of the four seasons, with frigid winters and warm summers.

One day, shortly after settling into his new life in Kabul, Christy was reading in his Bible and came across Acts 18:3—"And because he was of the same craft, he abode with them, and wrought: for by their occupation they were tentmakers." Paul had worked as a tentmaker in

Kabul in 1951
Courtesy of the Wilson family

Corinth nineteen centuries earlier so that he could serve as a self-supporting witness. And now Christy was working as a teacher in Kabul so that he could do the same. He was a modern-day tentmaker.

The power of tentmaking became a central theme in Christy's life, ministry, and teaching. Many years later, he was one of the founders of a ministry called Tentmakers International. He also authored a book titled *Today's Tentmakers,* the purpose of which was to "inspire, inform, encourage, and challenge those whom God is calling to serve as his tentmakers, his self-supporting witnesses around the world. [The book] also seeks to acquaint the Church with the unprecedented opportunity Christian lay people have of engaging in their professions abroad while at the same time being ambassadors for Christ."

Long before all of this, Christy served as a tentmaker when he began his four-and-a-half-year teaching career in Kabul. An English teacher had just left Habibia High School, and Christy's salary from the Afghan government would not start until he began teaching, so Howard Larsen asked him to get started immediately.

At Habibia, Christy taught English to four classes of thirty students each and provided administrative leadership. The Afghan people have a saying that one's teacher is his second father, and

Christy felt warmly accepted and appreciated by his new students. He quickly endeared himself to them by telling them about his adventures traveling from America to Afghanistan.

Habibia High School in Kabul, where Christy taught English
Courtesy of the Wilson family

However, Christy soon learned that the police were paying one student in each of his classes to inform them if he made any anti-Islamic remarks. "Sir, what do you think of Muhammad?" they would ask, trying to trick their new teacher.

"Excuse me, this is an English class," Christy would reply. "You can ask that of your theology professor, who is a mullah."

Christy's students were constantly cheating, and, as he reflected wryly, the only sin they saw in it was in getting caught. To prevent cheating during exams, some of which lasted up to three hours, Christy would place the chairs as far apart as possible and wander around the classroom with a watchful eye. He would also turn each exam into a personal prayer time, praying silently for each student by name.

"Lord, help this student to hear the gospel," he would intercede as he walked around the classroom, praying the same prayer for each student. Then the next time around the classroom, he would pray, "Lord, when this student hears the gospel, open his heart to believe." Each English exam afforded Christy the opportunity for a time of deep intercession.

During his first three months in Afghanistan, Christy led one of his fellow American teachers at Habibia, Charlie Motsch, to Christ. Christy and the other Christian teachers would gather together early each morning to pray for their students, as well as for the country. Despite the repression that kept them from speaking of Christ, no one could take away their freedom to pray.

Christy reflected, "We also had the freedom to show the fruit of the Holy Spirit: love, joy, peace, and so on. The Scriptures say: 'Against these there is no law.' No country can say you can't love, or you can't be joyful, or you can't have peace! And people saw the difference in the lives of Christians in Afghanistan."

When Christy and Betty first arrived, they lived in the home of Howard Larsen and his family. Eventually they found a place of their own on the edge of Kabul. Like virtually all homes in Kabul, it was surrounded by a wall high enough that the house was not visible from the street. However, anyone peeking through the gate would see gardens, fruit trees, and possibly a child playing in the garden.

Their new home had a painted cement floor and a flat roof constructed of a combination of mud and straw. When a heavy rain poured down on the single layer of mud on the roof, the house leaked terribly. Christy and Betty soon discovered the remedy for a drenched house: they stretched a bed sheet over the ceiling and hung a long string from the center of the sheet. Any water infiltrating the mud roof gathered at the center of the sheet, wound its way down the dangling string, and collected in a bucket below. During the heavy snowfalls of winter, the first priority for shoveling was always the roof.

Before long another tentmaking opportunity was presented to Christy, this one unique. It was April of 1952, and Christy had been in Afghanistan for only nine months. He was gradually assimilating into the life and culture of the Afghan people. He had loved these rugged and independent people from a distance his entire life; he was now growing to love them while living among them.

Sixteen months earlier, Howard Larsen had begun tutoring the crown prince, Ahmad Shah, on a weekly basis. But on April 21 Howard introduced him to Christy, and Christy soon found himself making trips to the palace to help the young man with his lessons.

Like many political families, the Afghan royal family had had its share of tragedy. Mohammed Zahir Shah, who was king when Christy arrived, had been thrust into his role at the age of nineteen when his father was assassinated at a high school graduation ceremony. The government immediately apprehended Abdul Khaliq, a man from the ethnic Hazara minority. They requited him by torturing and then executing him along with other potential rivals who may have helped plot the assassination. On November 8, 1933, the very day of the king's shooting, his son assumed the throne.

Ahmad Shah was the seventeen-year-old son of King Mohammed Zahir Shah. He was in the eleventh grade at the French School in Kabul, and Christy described him as "a very pleasant boy." He was the first in line of succession to be king, the heir apparent to the throne of Afghanistan.

Mohammed Zahir Shah

Two days after Christy and Ahmad Shah met, he wrote to his parents:

> Also please remember me as I have just started tutoring the Crown Prince in English twice a week. This is a great responsibility and I feel very humble and unqualified. I went to the Palace for the first time [the] day before yesterday with Howard and met His Excellency. He seems like a very fine young man.

Three months later Christy provided more details about tutoring the crown prince:

> I go to the Palace, one or two afternoons a week. They send a car and chauffeur for me. The Palace is very beautiful inside with tremendous marble pillars and floors, on which stretch long Turkman rugs in deep reds and blues. I walk up to the second floor on a gigantic stair case of 50 steps. There I either go to the Prince's suite, or else if it is warm we sit on a high porch. The furniture is beautiful inlay wood. There are also stuffed elephant feet which are used

as stools, and on the walls there are stuffed deer heads. After a few minutes of lesson, the servants bring in a table all set for tea with all kinds of fruits and cakes on it. We then have tea together, but can only eat a tenth of what is on the table. The lesson then continues a bit longer until the time for the Prince's evening prayer, around 6 P.M. He then excuses himself for around five minutes for his prayer. I also make this a special time of prayer. After this we continue our lesson for about an hour longer, and then I am driven home. I feel very unworthy of this privilege, but the effectiveness depends on your prayers.

However, the crown prince was not the only person of influence whom Christy taught. In March 1954 he was asked to teach a special English class to members of the Ministry of Foreign Affairs. He remained in that role until 1961, enabling him to become personally acquainted with many of Afghanistan's future leaders. Among his students was Noor Ahmad Etemadi, who served as Afghanistan's prime minister from 1967 to 1971.

Christy and Betty returned to the United States sporadically for brief visits. Occasionally issues crossed the officials' desks at the US embassy that could have jeopardized the Wilsons' return to Afghanistan, but Christy's former students from the Ministry of Foreign Affairs who worked in the embassy always stood up for the Wilsons and facilitated their return trip to Kabul.

Christy's teaching skills afforded him yet another service to the government of Afghanistan. King Mohammed Zahir Shah wanted to establish a constitutional monarchy patterned after England. To accomplish this goal, he needed to train young Afghan men to form the new government, and this required sending them to the United States or Europe for a formal education. Christy, along with several others, taught these young men the basics of English so they could attend universities in the United States and then return to Afghanistan.

Christy quickly discovered that the Afghan people were generally event-oriented but not time-oriented, and therefore few Afghans knew how old they were or when they had been born. However, when seeking to relocate to the United States, having a proper birth date is essential. To rectify this problem, Christy decided to assign each of these young men a birthday of his very own. "Your birthday will be January 1," he told one, "and your birthday will be December 25," he told another. "Your birthday will be July 4"—and so on until he had finished. "When you get to the United States, you will be celebrated!" he told them, trying to hide the grin on his face and the chuckle in his voice.

When the day came for a new group of students to journey to the United States, Christy sometimes accompanied them as far as he could. On August 31, 1955, he traveled with a cohort of students to Tehran. The students boarded a westbound plane to continue their long journey to the US, and Christy got on a flight back to Kabul to continue his teaching and administrative duties.

However, the plane never made it to Kabul. And Christy prepared for what appeared to be his final hours on earth.

CHAPTER 8
CLOSE CALL
OVER KANDAHAR

Then call on me when you are in trouble, and I will
rescue you, and you will give me glory.
Psalm 50:15

As Christy was flying home from Tehran to Kabul, he realized that some-
thing had gone dreadfully awry and survival was now in question. Since
Christy was a masterful storyteller, this chapter is taken from his own
telling of the events in More to Be Desired Than Gold *(see the notes for*
a full citation).

• • •

Glancing at my watch, 6:05 p.m., August 31, 1955, I knew something was wrong. We should have been preparing to land by now.
I peered out of the Iran Air DC 3 window, expecting to see the
familiar barren mountains surrounding Afghanistan's capital and
largest city—Kabul. But below stretched pine forests, valleys and
rugged mountains as far as the eye could see.

Suddenly I realized we were lost! Kabul was at least one hundred miles from the nearest forest.

Sitting at the controls of the plane were two Americans. The
pilot had never been in Afghanistan, and the co-pilot was serving
as guide without the aid of today's sophisticated navigational equipment. This was only his second flight through the Afghan skies.

Somewhere during the course of the scheduled one-hour and
forty-five minute flight, our pilot had made a wrong turn. I guessed
from the topography of the terrain below that we were probably over

the Afghan province of Khost, headed toward Nuristan and the Russian-Chinese border.

I swallowed hard. We were flying without any place to land over the jagged Central Asian wilderness.

Towering mountains soon dwarfed our small prop plane, with its unpressurized cabin. Banks of pink, billowy clouds loomed thousands of feet above us on the distant horizon. Then the twilight completely disappeared over the edge of the earth behind us. We seemed to be flying into an endless sea of blackness.

I was on this flight because I had accompanied a group of Afghan students to Tehran, Iran. They had boarded a westbound plane to continue their long journey to universities in the United States. Now, I was returning to Kabul to continue my teaching and administrative duties at Habibia College, one of Afghanistan's oldest and most respected schools for high school age boys.

Lost in my own thoughts, I wondered what else could go wrong. Mechanical difficulties had caused a two-hour delay in our departure that morning from Tehran's Mehrabad Airport. Then Iranian customs officials at Zahidan, near the southwestern tip of Afghanistan, had delayed us even further when they insisted that all baggage be taken off the plane and inspected.

The sun was already hanging low in the sky when we had reached our next stop—Kandahar, Afghanistan's largest southern city. We had dropped off about a half-dozen passengers, and before long we were speeding down the Kandahar runway for the final 300-mile leg of our flight.

At 4:20 p.m., our pilot had been confident that by dusk we would be taxiing toward the small Kabul terminal. But somewhere over Ghazni, he had followed a road heading northeast, paralleling the Pakistan border, instead of taking the northerly route to Kabul.

The more I thought about it, the more I realized the next few hours could very well be my last on earth.

I knew there were no night landing facilities in Afghanistan, or anywhere else within range. I also knew that the front baggage compartments were stashed with four-gallon cans filled with aviation fuel for the return trip—a necessity since fuel was not always available. A crash meant certain death in a blazing inferno.

I sensed a deep spiritual responsibility to speak with people on the plane about their relationship with God. Most passengers I talked to were very receptive. One American, however, cut me short saying, "Don't talk to me about that. When my time comes, it comes. And that's all there is to it!" He then turned away and continued to stare out the window into the night.

I then started a conversation with the Iranian steward. He responded: "I've been to Mecca. Doesn't that make me all right?"

I told him that the important issue now was not where he had been, but where he stood now in his relationship with God. If he repented of his sins and believed that Jesus had died on the cross in his place, then he would receive God's forgiveness. The steward seemed very receptive to what I was saying because he, like the others on the plane, was very frightened. He knew that the odds of coming out alive were against us.

A little later the steward gave me permission to enter the cockpit. I learned that the only radio contact the pilot and co-pilot had had was with Tehran, about 1300 miles to the west, and Karachi, Pakistan, an equal distance to the south. (Afghanistan airports were not yet radio-equipped.) The pilot banked the plane sharply to the left, completed a 180-degree turn, and started to follow the flight log in reverse.

It was the only solution he could think of.

When I mentioned I was a Christian minister, the co-pilot glanced over his shoulder and said, "Use all the influence you've got!"

"I'm praying," I answered. "And I know that God is in charge."

I returned to my seat and began to pray. I placed the fifteen people on the plane in God's hands. Then I pulled my Bible from my briefcase and wrote this note on the inside front cover:

Dearest Betty, Nancy, Christy, and Martin,

Our pilots have lost their way, and it appears that we will crash. I am writing this farewell message in case my Bible is found in the wreckage. I love you more than words can tell.

Put Jesus first throughout your life and serve Him faithfully in every way you can. I look forward to seeing you again soon in Heaven.

Your loving husband and dad,
Christy

I had just finished signing the note when from the corner of my eye I caught a glimpse of something coming up over the left wing. A beautiful full moon was rising over the eastern horizon, illuminating the mountains and valleys. God brought this miracle of timing just when we needed it. We had finally come out of the ominous clouds into clearer night air. The pilot then kept flying by moonlight.

I went back to the cockpit and scouted the silver landscape below. The terrain looked vaguely familiar. I soon recognized a village I had driven through only ten days earlier when I had traveled the bumpy road from Kabul to Kandahar for the funeral of an American engineer. He had drowned in the Helmand River while helping to build a dam.

"That town down there is Qalat!" I said to the pilot over the engine's roar. I remembered that Qalat had a spring of water which stands within an adobe fort on a hill like an acropolis. The co-pilot checked the map and found our location. From there we headed for Kandahar.

My prayers had been answered.

8:30 p.m. We could see the glow of Kandahar's lights in the distance. But the joy I felt was short-lived. Some quick arithmetic told me we had been airborne for more than four hours. We would soon run out of fuel.

No sooner had this thought crossed my mind than the co-pilot spoke up: "We've got to get the airport lit up before we can land!"

"I don't think there is so much as one light bulb at the airfield," I replied softly, hating to reveal the gravity of the situation.

The pilot turned to look at me. "If we can't get it lit up, we'll have to continue flying until we reach Iran!" Then he added solemnly, "But we don't have enough fuel to make it."

How ironic! Even though we had jerry tins of extra gasoline on board, there was no way to fuel the plane while in flight.

Soon we reached the outskirts of Kandahar, and I sighted the Morrison-Knudsen Construction camp. This company had been contracted by the Afghanistan and United States governments to build an irrigation system in Afghanistan's Helmand Valley. During the 1950s, two dams were erected and hundreds of miles of irrigation ditches were dredged in an effort to help the Afghans produce more food in their arid climate. Patterned after the Tennessee Valley Authority, this project had involved hundreds of Americans at one time or another.

I pointed out the location of the camp to the pilots.

"Why don't we fly low over the camp?" I suggested. "Planes don't fly into Kandahar at night so the noise of the engines will attract attention. The construction workers may realize we're in trouble and figure out a way to help."

The pilot made three passes as low as he dared.

Within minutes, many jeeps, cars, and trucks at the site were racing to the airfield. Light from their headlights flooded the runway as the vehicles lined up on each side of the gravel strip!

The landing was perfect!

By the time the flight attendant could lift the latch and open the cabin door, our "welcoming committee" had gathered to greet us. Several of us couldn't wait for the steward to roll down the portable stairs. We leaped out the open door to the ground below, into the midst of the jubilant American workers. No one had ever looked so welcome as these men who had saved our lives!

One husky American engineer recognized me.

"Christy, you mean to say you were on that plane!" he said incredulously. Then he engulfed me in a bear hug I shall never forget. We had become acquainted on my recent visit to Kandahar. Not only had I conducted funeral services for his friend, but I had baptized his daughter as well.

Morrison-Knudsen's director, T. Y. Johnson, invited all the passengers and crew to a steak dinner at the construction camp. To top it off, they served strawberry shortcake for dessert. Our unexpected hosts also rolled out every spare cot and bed on the grounds, doing their best to convert their simple accommodations into a first-class hotel. The Waldorf-Astoria it was not. But we did not care. We were all happy just to be alive.

The next day, September 1, 1955, dawned bright and clear. After a hearty breakfast, the construction crew chauffeured us all back to the airport. They refused to take a penny for their hospitality.

My mind again began to wander as we gained altitude and the DC 3 propellers spun us toward Kabul for the second time.

Never had I been more grateful for answered prayer. God's words in Psalm 50:15 were even more meaningful now:

> *I want you to trust Me in your times of trouble,*
> *so I can rescue you and you can give Me glory.*

Time and time again, God had reaffirmed my decision to bring my wife Betty to this mountainous, out-of-the-way country in the heart of Central Asia where our three children had been born and raised. I had been ready to die to go to be with Jesus. But the miracle of the previous evening had confirmed that God indeed wanted me working and living among these freedom-loving people in Afghanistan, where later we saw the Lord give spiritual fruit and had many other experiences of God's gracious providence.

CHAPTER 9
A FATHER'S JOY

Fathers, do not provoke your children to anger by the way you treat them. Rather,
bring them up with the discipline and instruction that comes from the Lord.
Ephesians 6:4

Christy always loved and respected his parents. However, he did not always agree with their decisions. Beginning in 1936, his father stayed on the Iranian mission field alone for more than three years while his mother returned to the United States with their four children. Their decision required tremendous sacrifice from each of them, and Christy later noted that he thought they should have come back as a whole family.

Furthermore, Christy knew that faithful service to the Lord guarantees neither a happy home nor godly children. He was well aware that an active ministry can sometimes lead to the opposite. He noted the tragic family life of Billy Sunday, the great evangelist of the early 1900s, and resolved not to repeat the same error: "Bob Pierce told me (and he had his own problems this way) that Ma Sunday had said to him, 'My husband led thousands and thousands to Christ,' but she said, 'all six of our children went to hell.' I think this is a danger of placing our work before our family and thinking our work is the Lord. And our work is not the Lord. . . . We therefore kept all three of our children with us all the way through high school as a family."

Christy made a clear distinction between the Lord and his work for the Lord. He had resolved long ago to place the Lord above all else, but he also resolved to place his family before his work for the Lord.

The children never felt that they were impediments to their parents' mission; rather they sensed that they were a vital part of it.

Psalm 127:4–5 says, "Like arrows in the hand of a warrior are the children of one's youth. Blessed is the man who fills his quiver with them!" Christy and Betty's quiver was full of adventurous children. Nancy was born in November 1951, Christy III (Chris) in April 1953, and Martin in December 1954. Each of the three was born on Afghan soil and grew up riding bikes and flying kites over the rugged, mountainous terrain of Kabul.

When the children were three, four, and six years old, a visitor to Kabul wrote home with a report of her adventures while staying with the Wilsons:

> Never a dull moment, oh yes: yesterday the kids had a birthday—Christmas party, too. I can recommend ministers' homes as rest homes only for those with an iron constitution. However, since Christy is a very spiritual man, I thought about "Thou shalt be saved—thou & thy house" and figured if the end of the world should come, I'd just be lifted right up into the air with the family, house & all—so what's the stomping of a few dozen little feet, the blowing of harmonicas, slamming of glass doors and such details when you have such security?

The Wilson family in Afghanistan in 1959
Courtesy of the Wilson family

Christy and Betty took seriously the Lord's command to bring up their children "with the discipline and instruction that comes from the Lord" (Eph 6:4). They dedicated each of their children to the Lord before they were even born. Each morning they awoke at five o'clock and spent the first two hours of the day in prayer and personal devotions. The children would overhear from their bedrooms as their mom and dad prayed for each of them by name, as well as for their future spouses, the church, and the Afghan people.

Before every meal Christy read a portion of *Daily Light* to his children. Each reading presented different portions of the Bible, arranged by themes, which he would then expound on. On the ragged pages of *Daily Light*, Christy recorded the birthdays of anyone who visited the Wilson home. This resulted in as many as five or six names being neatly written for most days of the year. As he read a portion of the book before each mealtime, he would also pray for anyone with that particular birthday.

At times these practices irritated his children. Sometimes they were impatient and wanted to get away; other times they stifled giggles. However, Christy remained faithful in this family discipline, and the Scripture passages stuck in his children's heads and hearts as they journeyed through their adolescent and adult years.

Christy also challenged his children with Scripture memory. "Who can memorize John 1?" he would ask them. "Who can memorize Psalm 91?" With each memory contest he offered prizes to those who were successful, allowing them to use any translation they chose. Together as a family, the Wilsons memorized John 1 and 3, Romans 12, Psalms 91, 100, and 121, and many other chapters of the Bible. Christy also encouraged each child to read the Bible for themselves and have daily personal devotions.

When Christy was in an important meeting, the children always knew they could run in and interrupt if they had a problem. Their father would pause the meeting and attend to their needs—which were often childish, yet no less important to Christy than the business at hand. One day, when Marty was six years old, he knocked on the door of his father's study. Christy was quite busy, but he opened the door, welcomed his youngest child in, and put his work aside. Marty knew from experience that he could always ask his dad questions and spend as much time with him as he wanted.

As Christy sat in his desk chair, Marty crawled up onto his lap. "Dad, I want to accept Jesus into my heart," he announced. "I love Jesus, and I want to accept him."

Christy and Marty talked for a few moments about what that meant. Marty understood God's love, because he saw it lived out in his mom and dad. Christy had Marty pray, and then the two prayed and read some Scriptures together.

A week later Marty came back and informed his father, "Dad, I want to accept Jesus again."

"Well, you did it last week," his dad replied gently. "But come on in. Let's pray and talk about it some more." Marty simply wanted to be sure.

• • •

While their dad's life exuded love and kindness, the children also knew that he was firm and sometimes exhibited a temper. When Nancy was in third grade, her father handed down the punishment of having to miss school the following day. To Nancy, it was a fate worse than any other imaginable, and she screamed in protest until she was hoarse. She hoped against hope that her father might relent and change his mind during the night. But when the following morning arrived, she was disappointed to find that his resolve had not softened one bit. And she did not go anywhere that day.

Before Christy's frequent drives to the airport to pick up guests, he'd announce, "I'm going to the airport; would anyone like to go?" Nancy usually jumped at the offer. She loved to be in her dad's presence, to have him all to herself, and to listen to the adult conversation during the drive home.

Once Chris and Marty also accompanied their dad to the airport. After the guest and his luggage were safely retrieved and in the car, Christy got behind the wheel and began to pray, as he did virtually every time he prepared to drive anywhere.

Suddenly, as Christy was praying, there was a strong earthquake that made the car bounce and shake. Suspecting that the two youngsters in the back seat were horsing around, Christy paused his prayer just long enough to turn around and discipline them. However, this turned out to be one of the few times they were both behaving. The truth emerged that the source of the disruption was seismic rather than horseplay, and Chris and Marty took advantage of their father's mistake for a long time to come.

Although the Wilsons' finances were limited, the children felt like they were part of the wealthiest family in the world. Each Christmas the Sears catalog appeared, complete with pictures of enticing toys. Their parents tore out pictures of the most desired treasures and took them to the bazaar. "Can you make one of these?" they would ask the merchants. On Christmas morning, the children were delighted to unwrap the toys they wanted most, handcrafted in Afghanistan for a very low price.

Another treasure Christy brought home from Kabul's bazaar was a mynah bird. The Wilson children enjoyed their pet for many years, marveling at its exceptional intelligence and vocabulary. Christy recorded words and phrases that he wanted the bird to say. He would place the tape recorder in the bird's cage, where it played repeatedly through the night. The children were startled the first time they heard the mynah bird address each of them by name; they were even more astonished when the bird whistled "Jesus Loves Me." When Afghan playmates visited, the bird spoke to them in their native Dari.

• • •

Christy possessed a healthy dose of mischievousness. One day his sons and their Boy Scout troop hiked through the nearby mountains in quest of a merit badge for history. Many years earlier, the British army had sought to retreat peacefully from Kabul by this route and had been told they would receive safe passage. However, as they made their way out of Kabul, they were decimated by Afghan gunfire. All but one were killed, the sole survivor spreading the news of the massacre.

As the Boy Scouts explored the battlefield, listening to the story of the British army's annihilation, Christy and a family friend decided to add a dose of realism to the history lesson: they would stage an attack.

Suddenly gunshots and yelling echoed across the battlefield. The troop of terrified Boy Scouts went diving for cover under cars. Shivering with fear, they wondered if these might be their final moments on earth.

After the gunshots had subsided, Marty and Chris peaked out from their hiding places and caught a glimpse of the culprits. "Ah, Dad!" they cried out. The young merit-badge-seekers had been the victims of a carefully crafted prank.

• • •

Christy wasn't one to lavish his children with excessive praise, so when he complimented them it was all the more special. Once during Nancy's high school years, when she was somewhat bashful and self-conscious, her father told her what a beautiful young woman she was. These choice words stuck permanently in her heart.

As Chris entered his high school years, he was eager to make friends. He spent some of his evenings drinking beer with other foreign teenage boys in Kabul. Christy was strongly against the use of alcohol, having witnessed on many occasions the potential for devastation from alcoholism and other addictions. When Chris came home drunk in the wee hours of the night, his father would greet him at the front door. "Chris, I love you," he would say, "and I want you to know that I'm praying for you." Unknown to Chris, however, his father was praying that God would give him a strong distaste for alcohol. Before long, that is exactly what happened.

During a particularly difficult season in Christy's life, he was accused of wrongdoing by other workers in Kabul. They set forth their accusations in a letter to Christy's church board, encouraging them to drop their support of Christy. However, the board chairman replied that they would not even entertain such accusations.

One evening Christy met with those who were opposing and berating him. It was a taxing conversation, and to make matters worse, the Wilsons' German shepherd had just died while giving birth to three puppies, and the family had to feed the three pups with a baby bottle.

As Christy came through the front door that evening, his family immediately sensed that he was exhausted and shaken. His grief and disheartenment were palpable. The Wilson children, who had always viewed their father as a rock, saw him for the first time as a man who was vulnerable. The family huddled together, prayed, and expressed words of love to each other during this trying time.

When Christy died in February 1999, his children crafted the following tribute:

DAD

He was a man in love with God. This love intensified his love for us and for people everywhere. His life was focused on sharing the love of God with the unreached. Dad lived at home what he preached outside our home. He inspired us to commit the word of God to memory and to apply it in our lives. He was our confidant, supporting us in the challenges of life, celebrating our joys and lifting us in times of adversity. He was a man of prayer. We knew with certainty that wherever we were, no matter what the circumstance, Dad was holding us up before the throne of God in prayer. He taught us never to give up or compromise what was right and true. In his life, sickness and home-going, he taught us acceptance of God's will, never complaining, happy with the little joys of life and continuing constant in prayer. He looked forward to that great day when we will be united in heaven to be with the

Lord forever. Until then, the love he showered on us and the example he set as a father and husband sustain us as we continue life's journey. Our hearts ache at his going but are lifted and strengthened by God's grace. And so, we commit our dear Dad and Husband into the loving arms of our Lord and Savior, Jesus Christ.

CHAPTER 10
TWO WATERMELONS
IN ONE HAND

*Care for the flock that God has entrusted to you. Watch over it
willingly, not grudgingly—not for what you will get out of it, but
because you are eager to serve God. Don't lord it over the people
assigned to your care, but lead them by your own good example.*
1 Peter 5:2–3

While Christy taught English to Afghans, they in turn taught him
some of their treasured proverbs. One of them was *Du tarbuz da yak
dest gerefta na mesha.* An English translation might read, "Two watermelons can't be held in one hand," meaning that if you have too many
preoccupations, you will succeed at none of them. Christy experienced
this pearl of wisdom firsthand as he sought to balance his teaching and
pastoral roles a few years into the Wilsons' time in Kabul.

When Christy and Betty had first arrived in the city, they immediately connected themselves with a group of other Christian
teachers. They dug deep roots of community, sharing fellowship
and praying together. Due to
Afghan suspicion of foreigners
and some uneasiness within
the American embassy, they
felt it wise to draw their cur-
tains and hide their Bibles lest
there be trouble.

The British embassy pro-
vided a vespers service on
Sundays, and when they

Vespers services at the British
embassy in Kabul
Courtesy of the Wilson family

learned that Christy was a pastor, they invited him to come and preach. As time passed, this small group of international believers steadily grew.

In late 1952, Christy and other teachers planted the Community Christian Church of Kabul (CCCK) for the foreign community. The church was birthed as an interdenominational congregation with an evangelical statement of faith. Christy was formally chosen as their pastor on November 16, and on December 21 the congregation gathered in the home of American ambassador Angus Ward for their first worship service.

The church's self-description included the following:

> We are people who come from many countries of the world to live and serve in Kabul. We have been delighted to find each other as we gather around our Lord Jesus Christ.
>
> Our desire is to be a twentieth century Church with a first century message. We have no special doctrinal twist, no particular denominational emphasis; we simply want to be Christians together.
>
> We take the Word of God, the Bible, as our guide and submit to its message. We hold the historic doctrines of Christianity and have experienced the grace of God in our lives.
>
> We invite you into our fellowship and ministry. Come, worship and work with us. It's exciting to follow Christ together.
>
> Every day we want to live with Christ. The Church in Kabul is not a building with gathered people but also people scattered—wherever Christians are all week long, there is the Church.

Each person who joined the newborn congregation testified to their conversion and assented to the church's confession of faith, and families were permitted to make their own decision regarding the timing and mode of baptism. As time passed, God used CCCK in the conversion of several within the international community.

Christy loved serving as their pastor; he loved teaching his flock and shepherding them. However, he soon found himself busy with weddings, funerals, and other pastoral duties for the international community. Sundays were especially demanding, since he had teaching responsibilities (his tentmaking role) in addition to the weekly worship service. Christy began to feel that this was simply too much for him—he was trying to hold two watermelons in one hand.

One Sunday as he was riding his bicycle to class, a bee stung his lip, and when he arrived in the classroom he could hardly teach his students. He took this as a sign from the Lord that he should seek Sundays off from teaching. Since Sunday was a workday for Afghans, he needed to obtain special permission not to teach then. He also had to be willing to accept the accompanying cut in salary.

However, after working for a season with his reduced teaching schedule of thirty-five hours per week, he still felt like he was taking on too much. He was essentially working two full-time jobs, and he simply had to decide between teaching English to Afghans and pastoring the international community in Kabul. His teaching position paid a steady and livable salary, while his pastoral ministry offered very little income or financial security for his growing family. Yet Christy clearly felt the Lord's leading.

A petition was drawn up requesting the Afghan government to let Christy remain in Afghanistan as a full-time pastor for the foreign community. The government granted this most unusual request, but it meant that Christy would no longer be paid to teach English. Because the church could not afford to support him adequately, a committee was formed to help raise the needed support. The initial committee consisted of Christy's father, a lawyer, and several other Christian leaders. Together they raised funds to provide for the Wilsons' needs in Kabul, enable them to go home on furloughs, and send their children to college.

So it was that Christy relinquished one of the watermelons in his hand and began to serve full-time as pastor for the international community in Kabul. It was a vibrant congregation, with people from many different nations of the world, and it continually grew as more and more embassies and aid agencies established themselves in Kabul.

Wilson family home and place of worship for CCCK
Courtesy of the Wilson family

At first the flock met informally in different homes on Sunday afternoons. When Christy and Betty rented a house with a large living room in the Karte Char district of Kabul, the growing congregation moved to their home.

A visitor to the Wilson home in 1956 documented memories of body life at CCCK:

The next day was Sunday and while Betty did her household chores, I did the flowers for Sunday service. It was really a very impressive sight at 3 o'clock in the afternoon to see these young American and European couples bringing their children. The tiny babies were laid out in rows on the guestroom bed, while the slightly older members were pushed by their fathers in their baby carriages and parked in rows in Betty's bedroom. The more articulate members went to Sunday School while their mothers and fathers came to church. Christy has made a very nice little chapel out of a room at the side of their house and I was surprised to find it attended by almost fifty members of the community. The whole service was very inspiring, and one got the feeling that these people were drawn together by a deep love of God. They could not have a more sincere person to lead them than Christy. I have never met anybody in my life who is on such intimate terms with God. No matter is too small to be referred to Him for help and guidance. And in this way he has not only won the respect of the European community but their devotion as well. He is doing amazing work in a country which is predominantly Muslem.

When Christy preached on Sunday mornings, he wore a long black robe with flowing sleeves, each sleeve adorned with three dark velvet bands. His shoes were brown and neatly polished. His voice could be easily heard; it was gentle, yet firm. His eyes were kind, with a sparkle, and he carried an authority that did not threaten but beckoned people to follow where he led.

As CCCK grew to include members from fourteen different nations, including China, India, Germany, France, Italy, England, and the United States, the multinational families enjoyed a strong sense of community. To foster a family atmosphere and teach respect, the children were encouraged to call all of the adults either "aunt" or "uncle."

One of the many duties Christy treasured was teaching a three-month class for expat teens from the international embassies and consulates. When they joined the church, he gave each one a life verse. One expat remembered that for her Christy chose Acts 4:12—"There is salvation in no one else! God has given no other name under heaven by which we must be saved." She learned that day from Christy that sin did not have power over her life because of the power of the name of Jesus.

Some of Christy's most impactful lessons for his flock were "caught" rather than taught, imparted by his life rather than his words. One such caught life lesson began early on school-day mornings when Christy would drive Betty to a kindergarten on the other side of Kabul where she taught expat children. Christy and one of his church elders, Cleo Shook, would then drive off together and be gone for several hours. When the two men returned, their shoes were dusty and their faces glowing with peace and joy. Years later the children learned that Uncle Christy and Uncle Cleo had been walking and praying all over the city and its surrounding residential areas. As they walked, they prayed for the land on which their feet trod and for the people living in it—that the Lord would claim them as his own children.

Prayer was the hallmark of Christy's life in Kabul, as everywhere, and he prayed as readily as he breathed. He carried in his shirt pocket a small notebook in which he would write names and prayer requests throughout the day. If there was any new cause for prayer, Christy would immediately stop whatever he was doing and pray. Sometimes when he was walking with a group he would begin praying for someone they were talking about. Sometimes he would turn to someone else and ask them to pray. Whether in public or among friends, usually without even closing his eyes, he would simply begin talking with Jesus.

As Christy's pastoral ministry grew, with competing demands on his time, he crafted a personal purpose statement:

> Purpose—
>
> To glorify God in the place He leads me which is at present here. This involves obeying Him especially in the final commission, showing forth by my life the presence & power of the living Christ, manifesting the fruits of the Spirit, ministering to physical & spiritual needs in as far as possible, devoting myself to effective fervent prayer, studying to improve intellectual grasp of realities as they exist in the Scriptures and in the world, seeking to share what Christ means to me as Savior and Lord, uniting in fellowship and worship with those of like precious faith, believing in the effectiveness of the Lord's working together with us according to the principles and promises of His word,

seeking to inform other members of Christ's body of needs so they too can pray effectively and thus share in the completion of Christ's commission and believing that what He has promised He is able also to perform.

One of the more unusual ways Christy shared in the completion of Christ's commission was by performing funerals for those in the expat community. Funeral services were held in an old British military cemetery in the absence of a churchyard or building. When a Canadian Christian died while serving in Kabul with the United Nations, hundreds of Afghans assembled to show their respect. Suddenly, in a land where proselytizing was strictly forbidden, Christy found himself proclaiming the good news of Christ's death and resurrection before a large gathering of locals seated in the open air. Following the service, the minister of education approached him. "That was the most impressive funeral I have ever attended!" he declared. "The mullahs I know do not know what to say on such occasions. Will you please write out everything that you just said so I can share it with them?" Christy gladly obliged.

Christy was also called upon to perform a funeral for a young Christian engineer from the Morrison-Knudsen Company who drowned while saving an Afghan (see chapter 8). Many Afghan officials were present at that funeral as well, held near Easter time. They were deeply moved by the words of Christ, "Greater love hath no man than this, that a man lay down his life for his friends" (John 15:13), and by the way Christy applied them to the Easter message.

However, with the exception of funeral services, Christy and his flock had no freedom to openly proclaim the message of salvation in Christ. So they remained busy obeying the command of Christ to help those in need. This served as an expression of God's love and tilled the soil of the people's hearts in preparation for the day when gospel seeds could be freely sown.

An early project by the church brought Long Island ducks to Afghanistan. Christy asked a church in New York if they could send duckling eggs by air to Afghanistan. After an eighteen-day journey from the US via Pakistan, the initial consignment of forty-eight eggs arrived in Kabul. Unfortunately, they had arrived in the middle of a 120-degree heat wave.

"I'm afraid they're all cooked from the heat," a church elder lamented. "But let's pray. If God could give us one pair, that's all we need." So the church prayed. They carefully placed the duck eggs under some setting hens. While it normally takes three weeks to hatch a hen's egg, a duck's egg takes four; however, the mother hens didn't seem to mind working an extra week of overtime.

Of the first batch of eggs, only three hatched—one female and two drakes. The mother hen treated them as her own chicks, but no doubt she was alarmed when they got near water and the ducklings dived right in.

The king permitted the ducks to be placed in his royal gardens. As Christy later described, "The one duck saw her duty and did it nobly. The first season she laid eighty eggs. The king was so interested that he put the royal seal on each egg and numbered them so they could not be stolen."

The white Long Island ducks were carefully placed in lakes and rivers throughout the country. They multiplied rapidly, providing much-needed food for rural Afghans. They were cheaper than chickens, they provided nourishment, and their feathers could be used to make down quilts and warm clothing. An additional, unexpected benefit of the ducks was that they ate the snails that carried a destructive germ that killed sheep in Afghanistan—sheep that were critical to the economy. The Long Island ducks became known throughout the country as "royal ducks," and they provided a great benefit to the national diet and agriculture.

The church also imported rainbow trout eggs to supplement the primary fish in the Afghan diet, a bony, poor-quality fish that tasted like mud. Christy again wrote to a church in New York, which contacted the Department of Conservation on his behalf: "Our minister *extra muros* [outside the walls] is interested in getting rainbow trout eggs for Afghanistan."

A reply soon came back. "We're happy to hear that Rev. Muros is interested in getting trout eggs for Afghanistan." (Apparently they thought the Latin term represented Christy's first and last name.) Notwithstanding this amusing error, the Department sent a shipment of twenty-five thousand eggs, and the church in Kabul imported more from Japan. After placing them in a freshwater hatchery, they transferred them to streams and lakes throughout Afghanistan, providing a nutritious, tasty alternative to the usual fare for countless Afghans.

Yet another project undertaken by the church was the introduction of the silk industry. Dr. Kinston Keh, a Chinese elder with the church, worked with the United Nations in Afghanistan. After more than ten failed attempts, he was finally able to import silkworm eggs that successfully hatched. He introduced his silk production techniques to farmers who were growing poppies for opium, and the farmers were soon making more money from the silk than they had made from the drug.

Not all of CCCK's enterprises were economic. Each year the church joined together with the people—and animals—of Kabul to create a Christmas pageant. It was held under the stars, with floodlights illuminating the host of nativity characters. A little stable was built, complete with a rustic manger. Mary entered the scene riding on a real donkey, and the shepherds came driving some twenty sheep and lambs. The wise men arrived on three enormous Bactrian camels decorated with trappings and many bells. And the three Wilson children looked forward to a new role each time—some years as angels, others as shepherds.

Several Afghans declared the Christmas pageant to be the most moving religious service they had ever seen. Others heard the carols and the Christmas story and said, "Why, how wonderful! Everyone in the city should hear and see this. We never realized that Christmas had anything to do with the birth of Christ!"

Afghan visitors became Christy's constant companions. On most days he found himself busy from morning until night. Local people knew that he was fluent in their language and cared about them. His typical day was filled with visits, phone calls, and requests for help. On most mornings he awoke at five o'clock to meet with the Lord, sensing that it was his only opportunity for uninterrupted time alone, but on days when he anticipated a steady stream of visitors, he arose a full hour earlier.

Christy could not have imagined the gospel opportunities that would come to him when he let go of his financially secure teaching job for an uncertain pastoral role. God kept expanding his ministry beyond Kabul, and over time he became a kind of circuit rider, flying out to hold services in other regions of Afghanistan with internationals working in education, construction, business, and agriculture. (He made a lasting impression in vegetable-scarce Kandahar when he stepped off the airplane with a bouquet of carrots for his hosts.)

Paradoxically, it was in stepping *away* from his teaching role, where he seemed to have more chances to live out his faith publicly, that Christy gained unprecedented freedom to speak of Christ. If he hadn't obeyed the Lord by serving the international community as a full-time pastor, he never would have preached to hundreds of Afghans about the resurrection—or written down that same sermon for a government official to share with mullahs. When Christy died to his original plans, God brought new fruitfulness.

CHAPTER 11
ADVENTURES

*Now all glory to God, who is able, through his mighty power at work
within us, to accomplish infinitely more than we might ask or think.*
Ephesians 3:20

The Kabul of the 1950s and '60s was very different from the war-torn
Kabul of later decades. Led by a monarchy committed to progress,
this mile-high city began to exhibit signs of modernization. Paved
roads and street lights appeared, and an increasing number of auto-
mobiles joined the bicycles and donkey-drawn carts on the streets.
The city boasted schools (for both girls and boys) and stores selling
an array of imported goods. It served as the cultural and educational
hub of Afghanistan. Yet for most of the world it remained a remote
destination. Few citizens of the West could even locate it on a map.

Beneath the new sights and sounds of a modernizing Kabul lay
the ancient capital: a quiet city of enclosed gardens, with the rem-
nants of a fortress wall snaking its way up a mountain. The city
was nestled within a narrow valley surrounded by the snow-capped
mountains of the Hindu Kush. An old cannon stationed on a hill
was shot off each day at noon to announce to the people below the
time of day.

The Kabul of this era, at the crossroads of isolation and open-
ness to the world, started to see a steady stream of foreign visitors.
Such was the setting for some of Christy's most harrowing and
miraculous adventures. Those who knew Christy best knew that if
there were any adventures to be had, he could usually be found near
the center of the action.

During the early months of 1964, a young foreign couple visited Kabul. Peter was the son of a prominent American official; he had met Gunnel, a Swedish woman, while in India. They both loved to explore the remote regions of the world, traveling mostly by bicycle. As they made their way through Afghanistan, they spent some time in the Wilsons' home.

When they were about to leave the city, Christy made it clear to them just how dangerous traveling within Afghanistan could be. Taking his warning to heart, Peter and Gunnel called him every day to let him know they were safe as they ventured away from Kabul. But one day Christy's phone didn't ring, and he started to worry.

He notified the ambassador, as well as the couple's parents, and waited patiently for a breakthrough in locating the missing couple. Eventually, however, as time dragged on with no apparent progress, Christy and his friends decided to take matters into their own hands.

Peter and Gunnel on the day they left Kabul
Courtesy of the Wilson family

RJ was an Afghan friend and a Christ-follower. Pretending to be a salesman of pots and pans, he scouted out various nomadic camps, searching for the last place the young couple was known to have been. His expedition confirmed the worst: Peter had been killed and Gunnel taken captive by the chief of a Kuchi tribe.

Christy, RJ, and another friend, Jim Cudney, devised a plan to rescue Gunnel, with Christy catalyzing the plan. RJ volunteered to spearhead the operation and recruited several other Afghan men to join him. The plan called for some of the rescuers to arrive at night and stir up a diversion on one side of the camp, at which time RJ would go in and retrieve Gunnel.

The party was equipped with a letter from Gunnel's parents and a photo of her home in Sweden to assure her that they were indeed legitimate rescuers. One of the men would whistle "A Mighty Fortress Is Our God" to help the others locate the escape vehicle.

Since the nine men were known in the area, they did not want to reveal their identity at any time. They were determined to prevent potential blood feuds or retribution from the nomadic chief, so they made a mutual pact that, if any one of them were fatally wounded, the others would cut off his head and take it with them, preventing identification of the body.

On Saturday, March 7, at 11:00 p.m., the rescuers set out on horseback, armed with guns, ammunition, tear gas, and flares. They reached their destination, about two hundred yards west of a nearby village, where they dismounted and tied off their horses.

When they reached the nomads' camp, one of them spotted Gunnel: she was dressed in traditional Kuchi garb with a small veil over her head. When she spoke, her accent gave her away as a foreigner. RJ considered grabbing her and taking her as quickly as possible to the horses, but he feared that this would get them all shot.

Suddenly there was yelling and confusion, and RJ heard a bullet whiz through his *tombans*, his loose-fitting pants. He shot a flare high into the air and five more into the pursuing group of nomads. He then lit another flare and fired it to the north, while the rescuers escaped south toward their horses. Three of the team were wounded—one with a bullet in his left shoulder, another shot in his left thigh, and a third hit in his right arm.

The flares and tear gas were good deterrents, and the pursuers retreated to the camp along with their captive. Meanwhile, the rescuers rode away on horseback until they reached the main road. Those who were unhurt cut the nearby telephone wires and removed large sections to prevent easy repair, seeking to delay communication of the Kuchis with the outside world. Those who were injured were taken by car to seek medical help. Soon after the first radio message reached Kabul that the rescue attempt had failed, Christy and RJ were reunited and spent many long hours debriefing and consoling one another.

Sometime later, Christy and his fellow would-be rescuers learned that Gunnel had been married to the Kuchi chief and had borne him a son. She thwarted subsequent rescue attempts, saying that she didn't want to escape and that her son would become the next leader of the tribe.

• • •

During Christy's early years in Kabul, a young Afghan man had become a new follower of Christ. He was discovered by the government and immediately imprisoned. For over a week he was placed in shackles, left standing in water above his ankles.

Christy called a meeting of those in the expatriate Christian community to be held in the home of one of the elders, chosen for its central location and large living room. For security purposes, their helpers were given the evening off, ensuring that no word of the prayer meeting would make its way into Kabul's bazaars. The assembled expats spent a long time on their knees. A young girl named Cathie was part of this meeting, and to her it seemed like many hours of devoted prayer.

Late in the night there was a cautious knock at the gate. Cathie's father thought someone had come to join them in prayer, so he sent her to answer it. But when she opened the door, there stood the young man for whom they were praying. Cathie immediately closed the door and ran back inside to tell everyone the news. She left him standing outside the gate, just as Rhoda had done when Peter was released from prison (Acts 12:3–19).

Since the young man was in grave danger, he was quickly welcomed into the house. He explained that he had been released under the cover of night for no apparent reason. He was cold, hungry, and sick, and he smelled terrible. But there he stood among those who had been fervently praying for his freedom. God had miraculously answered their prayer. The people soon found a way to smuggle the young Afghan believer out of the country, and Cathie was nicknamed Rhoda for a very long time.

In another incident, Christy was called to a village he had previously visited. The village leader had a son who was in great danger. Christy discerned that it was a case of demon possession, and he asked the father if he could pray for the boy in the name of Jesus. (While Muslims consider Jesus—or Isa as he is called in the Quran—to be a prophet, they do not consider him to be the Son of God, nor do they pray to him.) The father gave Christy permission. After an extended time of prayer, as well as fasting, the demon was cast out, and the boy was once again in his right mind.

The testimony of such answers to prayer was powerful, yet they were seldom shared openly because of the great danger for the Afghan nationals involved.

One day Christy answered a knock at the door of his home. There stood a young Afghan he had just met, his face displaying an unusual blend of anguish and anticipation. The young man's brother had recently been martyred for his faith in Christ, the victim of a sabotage that led to his plane crashing during a solo flight.

"You know, I've had a very strange dream!" the Afghan proclaimed to Christy. "In this dream I saw my dead brother alive in a beautiful garden across a stream. There was wonderful fruit in that garden, and it looked so good that I asked my brother to give me some of that fruit. My brother answered that he was sorry but he couldn't. But he told me to come to your home and ask your family, and that you would tell me the way to that garden! And he told me that I could come there myself and have all the fruit I want. I've seen my brother in heaven! He sent me to your home! You must have the truth. What is it?"

When Christy told this young man the gospel, he accepted the Lord on the spot. He went on to do even more for the Lord than his martyred brother had done. He suffered for his commitment to Christ, being given electric shocks in an attempt to make him deny his faith.

• • •

In addition to local leaders and believers, Christy and his flock also ministered to a growing group of foreign hippies. During the tumult of the late '60s and early '70s, thousands of young people blazed a trail from Europe to Nepal and back again, passing through Turkey, Iran, Afghanistan, Pakistan, and India on the way. Kabul became one of the meccas along this "hippie trail." There were some unwelcome byproducts of this increased traffic: a growing drug culture with many overdoses and deaths, and young women descending into prostitution to support their addictions.

CCCK recognized its opportunity and responsibility to help these young people back onto a positive path. As Christy later reflected, "So began a saga that ended with one of the most unusual ministries I've ever had the privilege to be a part of." The church reached out to several other ministries, including the Salvation Army, Teen Challenge, and Youth With A Mission (YWAM), to forge a partnership in ministering to these lost travelers. In July 1970, YWAM sent a team of nine workers to Kabul, and the following summer fifteen more arrived. Partnering with them, CCCK rented the top two floors of a hotel in the heart of Kabul. Thus began The Way Out, a burgeoning ministry that offered temporary refuge to starving and drug-laden hippies while they returned to sobriety. The rules of behavior in this transitional living space were clearly presented as residents ascended the ninety-two steps of the hotel:

> No smoking of any kind.
>
> No immorality or bad language allowed.
>
> Anyone who does not abide by these regulations will have to leave.

The Way Out offered hope to desperate young people, and many came to Christ through this unique ministry. YWAM staff soon realized the need for a separate place where these new Christ-followers could live untethered from the influences of the drug culture. This new home became known as *Dilaram*—Dari for "heart's peace." Over time, thirty or forty young people from Dilaram connected themselves with CCCK. YWAM staff worker Floyd McClung, who traveled the "hippie trail" witnessing to young people and later joined hands with CCCK in ministering to them, reflected on this unusual Christian community:

> In the language of the Trail, they [members of CCCK] were "superstraight"—almost without exception—the very epitome of establishment roles and identities. Dr. Wilson and some of the leaders may have shared a vision for outreach to the rebellious young Westerners who were flooding into Kabul, but to most the idea of flinging wide open the church doors to these "dirty, diseased, long-haired layabouts" was a revolutionary and frightening idea. . . . The gap between the diplomats and the hippies was wide—morally, culturally, and spiritually. When church members were persuaded to attempt to span that chasm, it was with some hesitation and considerable anxiety on both sides.[1]

During one worship service, eight young men and women from Dilaram were baptized. Christy would never forget that day. It was a beautiful display that the "straights" of CCCK and the new Christians from the "hippie trail" could learn to accept, love, and care for one another. Like Christy, Floyd was struck by the unlikely oneness revealed in that event:

> It didn't happen overnight, but by that autumn afternoon when we arrived at the shore of Karga Lake for the baptismal service, it was deepening. About twenty-five of us in beads and sandals were met by a crowd of about seventy-five Community Church members in business suits and dresses who had come to join their Christian brothers and sisters in an emphatic testimony to the presence of Jesus Christ in

---

1. Floyd McClung, *Living on the Devil's Doorstep: From Kabul to Amsterdam* (Seattle: YWAM, 1988), 67.

Kabul. We were absolutely thrilled at their act of support. Though we may have seemed an incongruous, even laughable, mix to any outside observer, I'm certain the gathering warmed God's heart.[2]

The first person to be baptized—a young German named Paul—waded out into the lake until its gray water reached his waist. Christy pronounced the blessing and dipped him backward, and as he joyfully emerged from the water, the weather abruptly changed. A dark, gloomy, wind-whipped afternoon sky shed a fresh downpour of much-needed rain, transforming into light blue sky and sunshine.

Those who lined the lake's edge—both hippies and straights alike—stood in wonderment, many crying softly, others praising God, and all sensing a powerful unity of God's Spirit. Suddenly one of the CCCK members broke the silence, noting to the person standing next to him, "Do you realize that this is the first public baptism to have been held in Afghanistan for over one thousand years?"[3]

• • •

As Christy's time in Afghanistan was reaching its end, a young musical group from the US visited Kabul. They were touring the Middle East and nearby countries, performing songs and witnessing to their faith. Included in their tour was a concert in downtown Kabul.

"This is a strict Muslim government," the team leader warned the musicians. "If you say the wrong thing, you could end up in prison and at the same time jeopardize every Christian who lives in this country. Memorize these words and don't dare stray from them when you perform."

When the night of the concert arrived, nearly a thousand Afghans came to listen. The team carefully heeded their leader's warning. That is, until one teenager put down his guitar and said to the assembled Afghans, "I'd like to tell you about my best friend, a

---

2. Ibid., 68.
3. Ibid., 65–69.

man named Jesus, and the difference he has made in my life." The team leader was outraged. He signaled wildly from the side stage for the renegade musician to stop his ad-libs, but to no avail. The teenager proceeded to tell the crowd all about how God had transformed his life.

Suddenly an amazing thing happened. The minister of cultural affairs, who had been in the crowd, walked onto the stage to respond. "We have seen many American young people come through this country," he began. "Most of them come for drugs, and most look like hippies. We have not seen or heard from young people like you. God's love is a message my country needs. How thrilled I am to hear you! You are a prototype for the youth of Afghanistan to follow in the future. I would like to invite you to expand your tour so that you visit every college and faculty and also give this same message on Kabul Radio. I will make it happen."

Dumbfounded by the official reaction, the team changed their plans and extended their tour in Afghanistan. Night after night, when each concert was over, Afghan youth crowded around the group of musicians with questions about Jesus, a personal relationship with God, and how faith in him could make a difference in their lives.

Finally, on the last day of their triumphant tour in Afghanistan, the musicians were introduced to Christy. He drove them to an unconventional tour site: the only cemetery in Afghanistan where "infidels" could be buried. Stopping at the first gravestone, one that was worn with age, Christy explained, "This man worked here thirty years translating the Bible into the Afghan language. Not a single convert. And in this grave next to him lies the man who replaced him, along with his children who died here. He toiled for twenty-five years and baptized the first Afghan Christian."

Strolling among the gravestones, Christy told story after story about the early Christian workers in Afghanistan. When the tour and the stories were finished, he turned, looked the young people directly in the eyes, and addressed them: "For thirty years, one man moved rocks. That's all he did—move rocks. Then came his replacement, who did nothing but dig furrows. There came another who planted seeds, and another who watered. And now you kids—you kids—are bringing in the harvest."

The group leader later recalled, "It was one of the great moments of my life. I watched their faces as it suddenly dawned on these exuberant American teenagers that the amazing spiritual awakening they had witnessed was but the last step in a long line of faithful service stretching back over many decades."[4]

Christy knew that, like those kids, he too was but one in a long line of faithful servants in Afghanistan. He may have also sensed that his time to pass the baton on to others was rapidly approaching.

---

4.   Philip Yancey tells this story in *What Good Is God? In Search of a Faith That Matters* (New York: FaithWords, 2010), 219–22. Copyright ©2010 by Philip Yancey and SCCT. Used by permission of Jericho Books, an imprint of Faith Words/Hachette Book Group USA Inc. Yancey's narration is lightly paraphrased here.

CHAPTER 12
AN ASSIST FROM EISENHOWER

The work ahead of him is enormous, for the Temple he will build
is not for mere mortals—it is for the Lord God himself!
1 Chronicles 29:1

It would not be long before Christy Wilson was declared *persona non grata* by the Afghan government. Students were becoming followers of Christ, and certain Afghan officials were determined to rid themselves of the corrupting influence who was behind all of this. Furthermore, the church building was a source of increasing tension.

The church building—the home of CCCK, and the only Christian church building on private property in all of Afghanistan—was a mere three years old. Yet it had already caused enough trouble to fill a lifetime.

It had begun as a dream seventeen years earlier, when the Wilsons' living room was rapidly becoming too small to house all of the foreigners working in Kabul who wanted to worship together. On some Sundays Christy found himself standing in a doorway, preaching to people filling four rooms on the first floor of their home.

In 1956, the community of Christian foreigners in Kabul began to pray for permission to build a place of worship. Then a year later, they sent a letter to the Afghan cabinet seeking permission to secure land and erect a building. Since non-Afghans were not permitted to own land, they requested a ninety-nine-year lease, similar to the arrangement provided to foreign embassies. However, their request was denied.

Meanwhile, half a world away (both geographically and culturally), President Eisenhower was busy leading a nation through the first frosts of the Cold War. He had already been in office for six years, and his days were filled with such concerns as civil rights and atomic weapons, Communism and a new global role for the United States.

Eisenhower had been baptized shortly after his inauguration, sensing his great need for God's guiding hand upon his life and his presidential decisions. He had also connected himself with the National Presbyterian Church in Washington, DC, pastored by Edward Elson. The president knew Dr. Elson from the days when Eisenhower served as supreme allied commander and Elson served as an army chaplain. After the German surrender, Eisenhower asked Elson to represent him before the ruling body of the German Protestant church to help determine how it would be rebuilt.

Christy also knew Dr. Elson, and when he learned that President Eisenhower had been invited to the opening of a new mosque in Washington, DC, he sent him the following note:

> Since a mosque has been built for the Muslim diplomats in Washington, on a reciprocal basis, we should have a church built here in Kabul for the Christian diplomats. We have no place large enough where we can gather. Would you please ask the President to request permission for this from the King when he visits Afghanistan?

Elson spoke to Eisenhower, and he agreed to raise the issue when he came. On December 9, 1959, the president met for four and a half hours with King Mohammed Zahir Shah. In addition to discussing the Soviet influence in the region and increased US aid to Afghanistan, Eisenhower also asked the king for his permission to build a church. After this brief visit, Ambassador Henry Byroade followed up on the request by keeping it before the Afghan government.

The following year the government authorized the construction. However, their authorization included an unwelcome condition:

just as permission had been granted five years earlier for the construction of a Roman Catholic chapel at the Italian Embassy, this church must also be constructed on some embassy's property.

Since the international Christians in Kabul wanted to build on neutral soil, this was very disappointing. They felt that constructing a church on any particular nation's embassy grounds would greatly limit their ministry within the rest of the international community. Furthermore, the mosque in Washington, DC, had been constructed on private land. So they appealed once more. While the government did not slam the door on the church's request, they asked that it be temporarily tabled and then renewed at a later date.

Six long years passed as one excuse after another was given to the church community. Finally, on June 16, 1966, the prime minister's office granted permission for them to secure property on a long-term mortgage basis and build their long-desired church. The cabinet instructed the Municipality of Kabul to approve the plans to construct the new building.

Immediately the people of CCCK voted to secure the property and build the church, and they were soon moving full speed ahead. One of their first steps was to secure the services of an architect. Thomas Haughey, the president of an architects' association in New Zealand, had visited Afghanistan to observe firsthand the Lord's work there, and he agreed to develop the plans for the new edifice.

The church's planning committee explored several alternatives for the building's size and style. Arabesque, Western, and modern architecture were all considered, and the final proposal provided a motif that complemented the surrounding mountains.

On May 29, 1968, after Mr. Haughey had completed his plans, the congregation voted unanimously to approve them. Adding to the approval, an Afghan architect who was in charge of citywide construction also endorsed the plans, noting that this was just the kind of church building he would have wanted for Kabul.

However, despite the enthusiasm, there remained many conflicts both within and without over the next two years of planning and construction. Some objected to what they viewed as an exorbitant cost, while others objected to the selected architectural style. Some wanted a flat roof rather than the more conspicuous raised roof, and still others questioned the need for a church building at all.

Complaints came from all directions, but the most clamorous voices were those within the international community. One prominent member had lived and worked in Pakistan, and he had seen firsthand the large churches that were now relics of days long since past. In no way did they represent the current economic or demographic status of Christians in Pakistan, he noted sadly, and he did not want to see this kind of mistake perpetuated in Kabul. He was also concerned about the new building's proximity to the Russian embassy, at that time a center of Communist atheism, and he feared that the bright turquoise roof would attract attention as aircraft flew into Kabul.

Despite the plethora of criticisms from all directions, the congregation's plans moved forward. And Christy mastered the skill of listening attentively to complaints and responding with kindness, graciousness, and a warm smile, all the while holding firm to his resolve.

Another challenge was finances, but again, the Lord provided in wonderful ways. The money that was needed to construct this new place of worship was provided by people throughout the world. A group of Christian students in Korea contributed fifteen dollars, a little church in Japan with only seventeen people sent ten dollars, and blind Afghan students gave some of the few coins they possessed. The wife of a diplomat from a Communist nation quietly slipped into Christy and Betty's home one day and explained, "I'm so glad that the Afghan government has given you permission to build a church. I'm a Christian, but I can't come to worship there because the secret police from my country watch me all the time. However, I want to make a contribution."

Finally, they were within $20,000 of the total needed to construct the new building, and they continued to pray for God's provision of the remaining funds. One day the church received an unexpected phone call from an American woman who had just arrived in Kabul. She was calling from the airport, she explained, and wanted to talk with Christy. Could he meet her there? Curious, he said yes and drove out to see her.

"I understand that you have permission to build a church," she began after they had introduced themselves.

"Yes, we do," Christy replied.

"Please let me see the plans," she requested. After studying the drawings, she inquired, "How much money do you still need to complete the building?"

"We still need $20,000," Christy answered.

"My husband has gone to be with the Lord," she explained, "and my relatives are taken care of, so I have been traveling around the world giving away my money before I go to heaven. I want to lay up treasures there. I don't want the government to get my money after I die, nor do I want my relatives to fight over it. I want to invest it for eternity. I'll provide that $20,000."

With this gracious offer filling the gap, construction soon commenced. John Reoch, a Christian engineer from Toronto, arrived in Afghanistan to begin the work, and the day of groundbreaking was finally set for July 1969. The bishop of Lahore, Iniyat Massih, was the first to ceremonially break the soil, along with Ellen Rasmussen, representing those who had previously prayed, witnessed, and suffered to bring the message of salvation to the Afghans.

The building was constructed in less than a year, and great care was taken in crafting many of the details. Exquisite alabaster stonework was provided by Afghan work-

Betty in front of the newly constructed church building
Courtesy of the Wilson family

ers. An American woman arranged patterns in marble to create biblical images such as the river of life and the burning bush.

Slabs of white marble, with natural markings resembling a dove, were intended for the church's front door, but that never came to pass; instead, two slabs were used to mark the graves of Erik and Eva Barendsen, who were martyred and are now buried in Kabul.

Cornerstone of CCCK's building
Courtesy of the Wilson family

At last, on Pentecost Sunday, May 17, 1970, the building was dedicated. Hundreds of people gathered in grateful celebration, including Christy's father and mother. Ted Engstrom, at that time the executive vice president of World Vision, and Jean Darnall, of the Festival of Light in England, delivered the messages.

Murray McGavin, a Christian eye doctor from Scotland, sang the words to Psalm 84: "How amiable are Thy tabernacles, O LORD of hosts. . . . Yea the sparrow hath found a house . . . even thine altars." Since the doors and windows had not yet been installed, sparrows had indeed found a house within this amiable tabernacle. They flew merrily around the inside of the building, traveling from nest to nest as Dr. McGavin sang.

Dedication of the church's new building
Courtesy of the Wilson family

However, the exuberance was short lived. Just eight days after the dedication, Christy received a court order from the Municipality of Kabul demanding that all construction activities cease immediately. It was prompted by the government's concern about any visible non-Muslim influence. In addition, tensions were running high after a newspaper editor had published a prayer for Lenin's soul upon the one hundredth anniversary of the leader's birth in the neighboring Soviet Union.

Demonstrators criticized the king and turned against the Afghan government, and the mullahs demanded the execution of the editor. Demonstration leaders were promptly arrested. Against this political backdrop, the government decided that they could not risk further public outrage with the construction of the church.

Though disappointed, the people of CCCK remained hopeful and viewed this new delay as yet another opportunity to deepen their faith in the God who had been so faithful to them. People throughout the world sent words of encouragement to the congregation; among the encouragers were some prominent Christian leaders, including Corrie ten Boom, the Nazi concentration camp survivor.

In April 1971, almost a year after the notice to cease construction, the government gave the congregation permission to add the finishing touches to the building.

Following the completion of the building, the congregation grew to over two hundred people at morning worship services. A dozen hippies traveling through Afghanistan decided to become followers of Christ and were baptized in the sanctuary's baptistery, leading an Afghan who was present to observe, "I saw the light of God on the face of those young people." Two weddings were celebrated in the new sanctuary. Even though the foreign community could not worship freely with Afghans, it was a wonderful thing to hear the word of God proclaimed every week on Afghan soil.

Meanwhile, within this overwhelmingly Muslim nation, tensions were growing between those who were determined to keep themselves pure from all non-Islamic influences and those who desired a stronger relationship with the West. These tensions erupted one Sunday morning in September 1972, when forty soldiers suddenly began to attack the wall lining the church property with demolition tools. Fortunately, Robert Neumann, the American ambassador, was able to quickly appeal to the king for help, temporarily restoring peace.

However, five months later, on February 25, the soldiers arrived once again without warning, having scheduled their unwelcome visit for a Sunday when Ambassador Neumann would be out of the country for a physical exam. This time they totally destroyed the wall.

The congregation learned that the mayor of Kabul had ordered the destruction of the church building as well. They gathered for an emergency meeting and prayed for guidance in handling this unexpected assault.

Hans Mohr was a German businessman who purchased most of the semiprecious lapis lazuli stone mined each year in Afghanistan. He was also a leader in the church. He went to the mayor of Kabul, who had been educated in Germany, to seek a reversal of the order. "If your government touches that house of God, God will overthrow your government!" he boldly proclaimed. His words would prove to be more prophetic than he realized.

Three weeks later, Christy received a message from Ambassador Neumann: "The Afghanistan government has informed me that they are preparing a list of around ten people who will be ordered to leave the country. I don't know the names, but I'm sure you and your wife will be at the top." Surprisingly, Christy and Betty were not at the top of the list—in fact, they were not on the list at all. Prime Minister Mohammad Musa Shafiq, the creator of the list, was a leading proponent for the expulsion of Christy from Afghanistan, but he knew that Christy had previously served as a personal tutor for the prince, and he feared that the king would overrule his decision.

Despite Christy's absence from the list, Ambassador Neumann informed him in no uncertain terms that he and Betty were now *personae non gratae* in Afghanistan—they were officially no longer welcome. Some powerful people in the country had come to fear Christy. Afghans have great respect for their teachers and will generally do whatever they say to do, and many of the young men Christy had taught had become wealthy and influential. Therefore, some Afghans feared that Christy had enough influence to lead a coup. Likewise, the Russians were afraid that he might be a CIA agent.

Although it was clear from Ambassador Neumann's report that the Afghan government wanted Christy gone, they knew that it had to be handled delicately, so they would not openly order him to go. The decision to leave rested solely with Christy and Betty. However, the ambassador warned emphatically, "Christy, the American government can no longer take responsibility for your safety in Afghanistan."

Those words would haunt Christy and Betty for the next several days. Uneasiness crept into their hearts. They sensed that their ongoing presence in Kabul would jeopardize other ministries, while their departure might take pressure off the church. During their morning devotions on March 19, they read in Deuteronomy 1:6: "The LORD our God spoke to us at Horeb, saying, 'You have stayed long enough at this mountain.'" They also read Jesus' admonition to his disciples in Luke 9:5: "And as for those who do not receive you, as you go out from that city, shake the dust off your feet as a testimony against them."

It was clear that God's time for them to leave Afghanistan had come, and on March 21, with the blessing of CCCK, they decided to depart as soon as possible. They would have but three more days to spend with the people they had come to know and love so well. Rather than packing their belongings, they chose to spend those precious seventy-two remaining hours praying with loved ones and with their fellow believers in Kabul.

At midday on March 23, the flock of Christians for whom Christy served as pastor assembled on the lawn outside the new church building. Together, they prayed for Christy and Betty. One of the church elders observed, "Some might think that the Wilsons are *persona non grata* here—on the contrary, in palaces and in the homes of the poorest, among all classes of people, high and low, scholarly and illiterate, Afghan and foreign, they are respected, revered, and loved; the common people welcome them gladly. In making so many friends, one can hardly avoid provoking suspicion and the enmity of some. This is no strange thing, it has always been thus."

Christy and Betty would always remember Saturday, March 24, 1973, as the day they departed Afghanistan, each carrying only a suitcase of personal belongings. They were leaving the land in which they had lived and ministered for twenty-two years.

As they made their way to the airplane, Christy shook the dust from his feet.

CHAPTER 13
A CHURCH BUILDING DESTROYED, A GOVERNMENT OVERTHROWN

God will destroy anyone who destroys this temple.
1 Corinthians 3:17

In the wake of their departure, Christy and Betty discovered two evidences of God's sovereign and perfect timing. First, about ten days after leaving, they received news that Christy's father was dying, and they flew to California to be with him for his final three days on earth. Second, they learned that a group of Muslim zealots had been plotting to assassinate them with a car bomb. One way or another, their time in Afghanistan was clearly over.

When the Wilsons left the country, they ensured that Afghan officials could see them board the plane and watch it depart. They were well aware that they were now unwelcome.

Their first stop after leaving Afghan soil was Tehran, where they stayed in the apartment of a missionary couple. A few days later they flew to Lahore. Providentially, they had arrived just as a Pakistani woman high in government was trying to get to America, and Christy was able to put her in touch with Bob Pierce, the founder of World Vision and Samaritan's Purse.

They then flew up to Peshawar, where missionary friends greeted them. Christy and Betty had arranged for some elders in Kabul to collect a few treasured books from the many they had left behind and to transport them to Peshawar in their own car.

Next the Wilsons drove up into the mountains near Peshawar, to a little hotel in the peaceful valley of Swat surrounded by lovely streams and countryside. They needed to gather their wits and regroup.

They also hoped that things would now clear up in Kabul and that the church building would be spared.

They were barely there one night when Christy received a telephone call from Cleo Shook with the news that his father was very ill. Within twenty minutes, he and Betty had packed up all their belongings and were driving back to Peshawar. They made arrangements for their missionary friends to come and get the car, and then they caught the first flight out of Pakistan.

When they arrived in Los Angeles, they immediately went to Westminster Gardens, a retirement community in the suburb of Duarte where Christy's parents lived. They were surprised to be greeted by Christy Wilson Sr., who was eagerly waiting for them in a chair on the front lawn. He was overjoyed to see his son and daughter-in-law, but he was so weak that his legs gave out as they returned to the house.

On April 8, Christy, Betty, and Christy's mother, brother, and sister were all with him. As Christy Sr.'s breathing became increasingly labored, Christy sat next to him on the edge of the bed with his arm around him. Christy Sr. looked up and prayed, "Lord Jesus, help me," and suddenly his face glowed with radiance. "I see Jesus, I see the Lord!" he exclaimed. No one else in the room saw Christ, but Christy Sr. did, and he could not contain his joy. After lying down again, he said, "O come, O come, Emmanuel!" and together they all sang the Christmas carol—even though it was April.

As he lay in his bed, he pointed to a cushion with the words "Happiness is a Grandmother." His voice trembled with excitement. "Real happiness is going to be with Jesus! I'm going to be with Jesus—today!" They all prayed together, each family member thanking God for this dear man and for all he had meant to them. Then they sang the Doxology together, and as they sang the final "Amen," Christy Sr.'s spirit left them, leaving behind a well-worn body with a joyful smile on its face.

Christy's mother turned to him and said, "Christy, wouldn't it be just like Dad to lead his own funeral?"

A neighbor who had heard the news soon arrived at their front door seeking to offer her condolences. Instead of finding a grieving family, however, she encountered a home full of people who had just witnessed the joy of a person who knows he is going to be with the Lord. Their joy was contagious, and she left uplifted.

Shortly after the memorial service for Christy Sr., two important pieces of news reached Christy and Betty in California. The first was a letter from a young gentleman seeking permission to marry their daughter, Nancy. The letter had traveled the circuitous route from the United States to Afghanistan and then back to the States again, where it finally reached its intended recipients. The second was an invitation from Gordon-Conwell Theological Seminary in Massachusetts asking Christy to join their faculty. This was to be the first of several such invitations from Gordon-Conwell over the next year.

Despite the offer from the seminary, after much prayer, Christy and Betty sensed that the Lord would have them spend the next year in Iran. They flew from California to Tehran, where they rented a third-floor apartment on a side street off one of the main thoroughfares of the city. It was barely furnished, but they bought what they needed, and people gave them furniture as well. The David C. Cook Foundation, an organization supporting ministry efforts that benefited Christians worldwide, provided a grant that covered their living expenses and enabled Christy to write a book during his year in Tehran. Christy's first book, *Afghanistan: The Forbidden Harvest*, told the challenging story of God's work in the resistant land next door.

Meanwhile, Betty found a job teaching first grade in the Henry Martyn School, an academy primarily for international children. Betty worked long days, catching the bus at seven o'clock in the morning and returning twelve hours later.

Some from the community of hippies, who had been so prevalent in Kabul during the Wilsons' years there, made their way to Tehran and ended up in Christy and Betty's apartment. Christy did most of the housework, shopping for food, cooking meals, and cleaning dishes, while the hippies provided very little help. When their landlady observed one hippie picking lice out of another's hair, she immediately evicted the young travelers, and word soon reached Kabul that they would not be welcomed in the Wilsons' apartment in Tehran.

As Christy and Betty settled into their new surroundings, they connected themselves with the Iranian Presbyterian Church. Politically, it was a tense time in Iran; the church often prayed for the shah, as there were growing rumblings of national discontent just beneath the surface. (Those rumblings erupted five years after Christy and Betty left, when the shah was overthrown in the 1979 revolution led by Ayatollah Khomeini.)

Although they were only in Tehran for a year, Christy and Betty built many close relationships. A couple on the floor below became fast friends, and a woman from New Zealand came to serve as Christy's secretary. They also got to know many local missionaries, frequently hosting tea in their apartment. However, Christy's primary task during this time was to write a book documenting the centuries-old struggle to bring the gospel to the Afghan people.

• • •

Meanwhile, a thousand miles east of Tehran, the Afghan government was continuing its quest to rid itself once and for all of the church building. CCCK formed a negotiation team consisting of Albrecht Hauser, a German; Dr. Jock Anderson, a Briton; and Bill MacIlvain, an American. Despite their ongoing efforts, the acting mayor of Kabul, Dost Mohammad Fazl, sent the following communication to the church board:

> From the morning of Wednesday, 23rd Jawza, 1352 (June 13, 1973) the roof of the church will be destroyed by the Kabul Municipality. The building, in accordance with the decision of the higher authorities, will be used by the Kabul Municipality for other purposes. From the above-mentioned day no one has any right to enter the building or premises

of the church. Whoever enters will be punished as a violator of Afghan laws. The final date above has been announced to you.

The church leaders stared at the page, incredulous, unable to mask their shock and disappointment. When they had collected themselves, they tasked the negotiation team with appealing to Prime Minister Mohammad Musa Shafiq. On June 11, two days before the scheduled demolition, the team wrote one last letter:

> We have deeply appreciated all the understanding, advice and practical assistance that we have been given by your government and its various departments in the past. Without the good will of your people, this building would never have been erected.
>
> If the problem has a political and religious dimension, as well as one of legality, then would it not be possible for the Royal Afghan Government to justify the presence of the building in this country on the same basis that the presence of a mosque is justified in Christian countries; that is, on the basis of respect for the religious feelings and personal rights of the small foreign minority?

Then, after describing the financial and legal implications of this act, they issued a final appeal:

> Is this holy place of prayer, which was consecrated in the sight of God, going to be destroyed? Will devout Muslims really feel that this is the way to treat the "people of The Book"? As Christians, we shall not resist: firstly, because our Holy Book commands us to pray for, honor, and obey those who have the power to rule over us. But, secondly, we shall not resist because, although this beautiful building is of great value in terms of the investment of money

and effort put into it, there are other values which we prize more highly—such as peace and good will among men, freedom of conscience, respect for the rights and beliefs of others, freedom to live, and to love, worship and obey Almighty God. To Him we submit. How can we, in all conscience "give" this building for its demolition since it is dedicated to the glory of God? We cannot of ourselves accept responsibility for such a thing, for we are only trustees of that for which others have given and labored. The action taken will be the responsibility of the Royal Afghan Government.

Their letter assured the prime minister that the keys of the church would be handed over on demand to his authorized representative on June 13. It concluded with the benediction "May God bless you and your country."

Christians throughout the world interceded for CCCK and sent letters of appeal to various Afghan embassies. Leaders, including Billy Graham, sent a statement of concern to the king.

CCCK after its wall was destroyed by Afghan soldiers
Courtesy of the Wilson family

Unfortunately, the various letters and appeals did not deter the government's resolve. They had determined that this building would never again be used for Christian purposes. On June 14, soldiers, police, and workmen with bulldozers arrived to raze the vacated building. First the roof was destroyed, then the walls and the cornerstone. The soldiers, however, seemed afraid to touch the Christmas star within the building, viewing it as holy and sacred; it would be the last remnant to come down.

The congregation offered no resistance but instead served the men tea and cookies. "This building does not belong to us but to God," they told the soldiers. "We can't turn it over for destruction."

Some of the soldiers had tears in their eyes. "We know it is not right to destroy a house of God," they said, "but we are under orders and have to obey."

Two reported features of the building captivated the Afghan officials who had ordered its destruction.

Final steps in demolishing the church building
Courtesy of the Wilson family

First, the church's translation system, used to interpret messages simultaneously into several different languages, was a mysterious conglomerate of buttons and dials, wires and lights. The Russian embassy, located a mere two hundred yards up the street, suspected that these "secret listening devices" were being used to eavesdrop on Russian conversations, and they complained to the Afghan government.

Second, rumors had reached the Afghan secret police that an "underground church" existed in Afghanistan. Therefore, while the workers demolished the church building, they carefully dug twelve feet below its foundation in search of this secret subsurface sanctuary—but to no avail.

Meanwhile, Christy and Betty were in the United States attending a missions conference in the Midwest. Christy was preparing for dinner when the telephone in their motel room rang. On the other end was Ray Knighton, the president of MAP International. "Christy, I'm afraid I have some very bad news. I just got a call from the State Department in Washington. Word from Kabul is not very good. Apparently, the Afghan government has authorized the destruction of the church building."

Overcome with grief, a flood of emotion surging through his body, Christy threw himself on the floor and wept. It just didn't make sense. Why would the Lord allow such a thing?

However, even through his torrent of tears, Christy was able to thank the Lord, knowing that God was still in control and that their labor had not been in vain. Christ's words in John 12:24 brought a renewed peace to Christy's troubled mind and spirit: "Truly, truly, I say to you, unless a grain of wheat falls into the earth and dies, it remains by itself alone; but if it dies, it bears much fruit." God gave Christy the gentle assurance that even though the building was being destroyed, God would somehow be glorified through this experience.

Betty later observed that this season of Christy's life produced in him a new measure of sweetness and humility. He had no doubt that he had been following God's leading, and the experience taught him how to forgive those who opposed him.

• • •

On July 17, two events occurred that would forever change the Christian church in Kabul—and the entire Afghan nation.

First, the troops completed their destruction of the church building and finished their demolition of its foundation. Any lasting traces of the building were obliterated or removed, so that no physical remnant of the church building remained. The church itself, however, remained strong and continued to meet in the Wilsons' former home, adjacent to what had now become a vacant lot. As time passed, the growth of the Kabul church required that the walls of their home be pushed out to enlarge the makeshift sanctuary.

Second, before the dust and debris from the church building had fully settled, the government was overthrown. Afghanistan had been a monarchy for 227 years, but that very evening, Mohammed Daoud Khan, the king's cousin and former prime minister, staged a virtually bloodless coup and established a republican government. The king himself, who had ruled for the past forty years, was in Italy undergoing eye surgery at the time.

The prophecy that CCCK's Hans Mohr had spoken to the mayor of Kabul four months earlier had indeed come to pass—all within a single day. And in the following years, changes in Afghanistan came swiftly, with sweeping impact: In the late 1970s a Communist government seized power, and in the resulting struggle, the Soviet Union sent armies to back the fledgling regime. This ignited a bloody ten-year conflict that finally led to Soviet forces withdrawing from the country. In the ensuing power vacuum, a fierce civil war broke out between various factions of *mujahideen* trying to take control. The fighting nearly leveled Kabul, and the chaos paved the way for the Taliban takeover.

These years of strife killed hundreds of thousands of Afghans. Millions more fled the country as refugees. One of those refugees later made his way to the Wilsons' new home in the United States and observed, "Ever since our government destroyed that Christian church, God has been judging our country!"

CHAPTER 14
BECOMING PROFESSOR WILSON

You have heard me teach things that have been confirmed by many reliable witnesses. Now teach these truths to other trustworthy people who will be able to pass them on to others.
2 Timothy 2:2

High atop a rolling hill in South Hamilton, Massachusetts, covered with colorful New England foliage and surrounded by centuries-old colonial homes, sits the campus of Gordon-Conwell Theological Seminary. During the 1960s, when Christy was seeking to build a solid church in Kabul, three other godly men—Billy Graham, Harold John Ockenga, and J. Howard Pew—were seeking to build a solid evangelical seminary in the northeast United States. Under their leadership, Gordon Divinity School and Conwell School of Theology merged to form the seminary. Ockenga became its first president, Graham served on its board of trustees, and Pew provided much of its early funding.

It was four years after the merger that Dr. Ockenga invited Christy to teach at Gordon-Conwell. By now his work in Afghanistan was well known to many Christian leaders throughout the world. Dr. Ockenga had known him personally since 1946, when Christy directed the first InterVarsity missions conference in Toronto and Dr. Ockenga, at the time a forty-one-year-old pastor of Boston's Park Street Church, was one of the speakers.

Christy's initial reaction to the teaching invitation was reluctance, not wanting to tie himself down to any long-term commitment and still hoping that God would open the way for him to return to Afghanistan.

Shortly after that initial invitation, Christy was asked to speak at Urbana '73, along with John Stott, Elisabeth Elliot, Paul Little, and several other leaders in missions and evangelism. Christy introduced the conference participants to the relatively new concept of tentmaking, presenting self-supporting witness as a new means for bringing the gospel to nations that were closed to traditional missionaries.

Among the attendees was a small band of professors from Gordon-Conwell, including Nigel Kerr, a professor of church history and missions and a fellow graduate of the University of Edinburgh. The professors sought out Christy and urged him to become their colleague. Christy's reply was simple and direct: "I would be willing to come on the condition that I would be free to leave any time the way to Afghanistan opened once again." And so it was decided.

In June 1974, Christy and Betty left Iran and returned to the United States for the wedding of their daughter. Shortly after the wedding, they made their way to the Boston area to find a place to live and to get acquainted with their new surroundings. Professor Kerr's wife, Julie, was a realtor, and she helped them find their new home. After looking at several houses in South Hamilton and finding none that appealed to them, Christy and Betty accompanied Julie to Gloucester, an old coastal fishing town about a half-hour drive northeast of campus. Finally, at 502 Washington Street, they discovered a little Cape Cod–style house complete with a guest cottage and a backyard abutting a tiny ocean inlet. The Johnsons, who owned the house, were seeking someone to house-sit while they were away, and the rent was exceptionally reasonable at only two hundred dollars per month. Christy and Betty knew immediately that this was the home they were looking for—not only was the location excellent and the house charming, but since they had left all their belongings in Afghanistan, they were grateful to find that the space came fully furnished.

The Wilsons enjoyed living out their gift of hospitality, welcoming many people into their new home. For many of his classes, Christy invited students to his Cape Cod house for evenings of fun and fellowship, and Betty provided an assortment of home-cooked food.

When their landlord, Mr. Johnson, died, Mrs. Johnson returned to Gloucester and lived in the adjacent guest cottage. Finally, when Mrs. Johnson died, her children decided to sell the property and give the Wilsons the option to buy it. However, after much discussion and prayer, Christy and Betty decided to let it go, and they

Betty and Christy in their home in Gloucester in 1975
Courtesy of the Wilson family

moved into Graham Hall, one of the student apartments on campus, where they lived for four years. Though it was much smaller than their home in Gloucester, they enjoyed having more opportunities to build relationships with students. Thus, Christy and Betty never owned a home of their own.

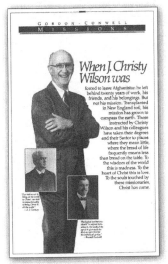

Excerpt from Gordon-Conwell publication
Source: Gordon-Conwell Theological Seminary

When Christy began his professorship at Gordon-Conwell in September 1974, he insisted on being known as a *visiting* professor, hanging on to the hope that he would one day return to his beloved Afghanistan. He also insisted that his title be "professor of world evangelization" rather than "professor of missions," feeling that this more clearly described his passion and his desired role at the seminary.

From the very start, Christy's prayer ministry was his joy

and foundation at Gordon-Conwell. He lived out his almost two decades as a seminary professor with the conviction that "there is such a strategic group of people here that if they are prayed for believingly God can use them in a mighty way to be a blessing not only to this country but to the rest of the world."

Every fall, Gordon-Conwell published a community directory with photos and personal information about each student, professor, and staff member. This was commonly referred to as the Facebook (long before this term was used for another purpose). Christy prayed through the entire Facebook each week, praying for each person individually. When students encountered him on campus for the first time, they would be surprised to hear a professor they had never met before address them by name. When Christy and Betty traveled, his Facebook went with them. Christy would drive, Betty would read the names to him, and Christy would pray. He also established a prayer room on campus, and every noon, he and a band of students united in prayer for the peoples and nations of the world.

In 1981, when Robert Cooley was inaugurated as Gordon-Conwell's second president, Billy Graham spoke at the inauguration. During his message and in many subsequent casual conversations, he strongly encouraged Dr. Cooley about the importance of a life of prayer and spiritual formation in leading the seminary. Dr. Cooley took these admonitions to heart, as he later explained: "I immediately established the discipline of daily prayer in the president's office. I invited everyone and anyone who would join me for prayer. My day began with prayer. I had one professor, J. Christy Wilson, who never missed a day during his time at the seminary in joining me."[1] He reflected further,

> Christy was a saintly man, dedicated to proclaiming the gospel. He was humble and unpretentious. Christy was a man of well-developed spiritual

---

1. Harold Myra and Marshall Shelley, *The Leadership Secrets of Billy Graham* (Grand Rapids, MI: Zondervan, 2005), 301.

disciplines. He made it a point to always introduce himself to strangers and to get to know them. Especially, he was committed to knowing the students. He would memorize every student's name and address them when in contact. Christy loved the people of the Middle East and the world, and he would seek every opportunity to speak about that world. And he was committed to evangelism, working hard to get the subject in curricula as a required course.

Christy's inspiration for launching a seminary course in personal evangelism had come while he was on furlough in 1969. During this time he participated in the North American Congress on Evangelism in Minneapolis, where evangelist D. James Kennedy was leading a seminar. Of more than six hundred pastors who attended Kennedy's session, Christy was astonished to learn that only three, or less than 1 percent, had been taught in seminary how to lead a person to Christ. In fact, looking back on his own education, he quickly realized that he had never been taught how to share the gospel by any of his teachers but rather had learned from a Christian layperson who was in the tool business. At that moment Christy determined that if he ever taught in a seminary, he would teach a class in personal evangelism.

Although Personal Evangelism was launched as an elective at Gordon-Conwell, hundreds of students enrolled in the course. One, a fifty-year-old pastor who had graduated from an evangelical seminary and pastored for a number of years, had never been taught how to lead a person to Christ, nor had he done so. As a result of the training and assignments in class, he brought the gospel to his congregation, and he was overjoyed to lead his first five people to the Lord.

In addition to Personal Evangelism, Christy also taught The World Mission of the Church, Effective Evangelism with Modern Religions and Cults, New Developments in Missions, The Christian

Approach to Islam, Missionary Anthropology Today, Reaching Unreached Peoples for Christ, and Tentmaking Witness at Home and Abroad. While these courses covered a broad range of topics, they shared several characteristics: stories of God's work wove their way through each curriculum and class time; students were required to memorize about thirty verses of Scripture; a normal reading list was approximately ten books; and grades were completely objective, based on each student's completion of the class requirements.

Christy's course The World Mission of the Church included a field trip to the Salem wharf where Adoniram Judson and four other missionaries had set sail for Burma aboard the *Caravan* in 1812. Another trip was to the field in Williamstown that had been the site of the 1806 Haystack Prayer Meeting, which helped launch the modern mission movement.

Like those earliest New England mobilizers, Christy during his Gordon-Conwell years would witness the sending forth of many fledgling missionaries. His role as professor would impact the far reaches of the world.

CHAPTER 15
ICE CREAM ON
THE CAKE

If your gift is serving others, serve them well. If you are a teacher, teach
well. If your gift is to encourage others, be encouraging. If it is giving, give
generously. If God has given you leadership ability, take the responsibility
seriously. And if you have a gift for showing kindness to others, do it gladly.
Romans 12:7–8

When Christy's former students share memories of their time with him at Gordon-Conwell, their stories all sound remarkably consistent:

> He would pray with you anytime and anyplace.
>
> He knew your name long before you knew his.
>
> He loved to tell stories of what God is doing throughout the world.
>
> He had a contagious smile and an infectious laugh.

In an article in *Christianity Today*, Wendy Murray Zoba reflects on her memories of Christy's classes at Gordon-Conwell:

> Anyone who took a class from Christy Wilson will remember two assignments. One was praying through prayer cards for all the nations of the world (available at the GCTS bookstore) and the other was writing a biblical defense for the exclusivity of

salvation in Christ and what that implies for Christian mission. Prayer and mission were his passions.

It was difficult to take notes when he lectured because his storytelling militated against it. He relieved our anxieties, though, by refusing to give any grade lower than an A-. So we sat back and heard his endless accounts of what *God did* in the course of Christy Wilson's remarkable lifetime.

He knew your name before you walked into class the first time. In fact, he knew your spouse's name and the names of your children. That is because he used to pray through Gordon-Conwell's student directory daily. This had the result of many students turning to him for guidance. As I walked through the hallways in the Kerr building, I would often see him standing off to the side praying with a student between classes. He seemed to be so intimately acquainted with the Lord. Prayer was everything to him.[1]

J. CHRISTY WILSON, JR.;
Professor of World Evangelization;
502 Washington St., Gloucester, MA
01930; 281-1192; Betty; Nancy,
Chris, Martin and five
grandchildren; fishing,
photography; UPCUSA. Ext. 553.

Christy's entry in the Gordon-Conwell Community Directory
Source: Gordon-Conwell Theological Seminary 1983–1984 Community Directory

Indeed, prayer and ministry were such high priorities for Christy that some of his friends felt he had little time for fun, relaxation, or close relationships. They observed that while Christy had many friends, he was intimate with very few.

---

1. Quoted in Michael Maudlin, "What Would J. Christy Wilson Do?," *Christianity Today*, April 5, 1999.

However, one result of Christy's single-mindedness was that students knew him as a man of deep prayer. Occasionally this inspired good-natured jokes. During one of Christy's classes a student fell asleep, and the student next to him poked him and told him, "Dr. Wilson just asked you to pray!" The sleeping student quickly woke up, stood, and began to pray in front of the entire class. When he was finished with his impromptu prayer, Christy graciously responded, "Well, thank you, brother, for those words of encouragement."

Christy himself had a good sense of humor. During his years at Gordon-Conwell, he started the Overseas Missions Practicum (OMP) to send students overseas and equip them with firsthand missions experience while in seminary. During a trip to Pakistan with a group of students, he negotiated the price of renting a Jeep. He still spoke beautiful Dari from his time in Afghanistan, so he was able to converse quite fluently with the Afghan man making the deal. He asked the cost of a rental. The man excused himself to seek out an answer, then promptly returned with a number.

Upon hearing the price, Christy replied, "Oh, I'm so sorry! My Dari must be terrible, because you obviously misunderstood me. You must have thought I asked the cost to *buy* the car."

In the summer of 1983, during the first practicum that Christy and Betty personally led, the team went on a ten-day trek up into the rocky mountainous area between Afghanistan and Pakistan. (This area, something of a no-man's-land, is the same region where Osama bin Laden is believed to have hidden before his move to the city of Abbottabad, Pakistan, where he was killed in 2011.)

The team hiked up into the wilderness to bring a gospel recording that Christy had worked on to the Kalash people. When they were six days into their journey, they spent the night under the open sky. Concerned that the locals might steal their fishing gear and poles, Christy asked Betty to sleep next to the equipment. However, sometime in the night Betty rolled over onto the poles and hooked herself. Christy woke up the team, instructing them, "We've got to go find a pair of pliers to break the barb off."

So the team went from house to house in search of pliers. Many of the local families invited the team members into their homes for a cup of tea. Eventually someone found an old, rusty pair of pliers, and the fishing hook was removed from Betty's stomach.

During yet another OMP trip to Pakistan, this one to minister among Afghan refugees, the team sought to bring a large solar oven with them on the airplane so they could give it to the displaced people. But the clerk at the airport terminal informed them that they would have to pay an additional fee of several hundred dollars to transport it.

"Well, let me pray about that," Christy said to the clerk. "Lord, you know this situation, and you know that the Afghan refugees need this solar oven." Right there at the counter, Christy continued to pray to the Lord, asking him to work in this situation and to provide a resolution. When he had finished praying, the clerk was either so impressed or so shaken that he waived the fee.

One of Christy's favorite pastimes at Gordon-Conwell was fishing. One year in June he found himself aboard the *Yankee Captains* on an all-night fishing adventure eighty miles off the New England coast. The waters were terribly rough, and everyone on board became seasick—everyone except a blind friend of Christy's named John Sanders. While John ate all the sandwiches on board, his fellow fishermen couldn't even stomach the sight of food. Christy had crossed the ocean a number of times, but never had he experienced such choppy seas. He was still sick two days after returning ashore.

On another fishing trip, he and an Afghan guest awoke early and set out to sea. One of the other fishermen caught something, but it got away, bleeding all over. The dissipating blood attracted a great white shark, which came up and swallowed the fugitive fish, leaving a boat of screaming fishermen.

Christy frequently went fishing with his colleague David Wells. During one outing, the boat happened upon a school of bluefish, known for their ferocious set of teeth. Dr. Wells caught a big one and put it into his gunnysack, which was tied to the railing. Without warning, the bluefish leaped out of the sack and onto the deck. Dr. Wells shouted to Christy to warn him, but since they were still surrounded by blues, everyone was too busy to pay attention. Suddenly the large, toothy fish leaped up and attached itself at hip level to Christy's blue jeans. Dr. Wells pulled and pulled, but the fish would not let go. After a few minutes of fighting with it, Christy said, "Enough of that! I'm getting back to the fish!" So Christy continued fishing with a seventeen- to eighteen-pound fish firmly attached to his leg. It was there for twenty minutes before it finally detached itself.

• • •

While at Gordon-Conwell, Christy and Betty connected themselves with Pigeon Cove Chapel, a little waterfront church in the town of Rockport. Christy's pastor and former student, Wayne Morgan, reflected that "Dr. Wilson believed, taught, and practiced that every Christian, though not an evangelist, is a witness for Christ. In his personal evangelism class at Gordon-Conwell Theological Seminary, we were required to witness to ten people during the course of the class. We had to share the complete plan of salvation so the person knew what they were accepting or rejecting. . . . Six of my ten prospects received Christ."

As a student, Wayne had once entered Lecture Hall #2 in the Goddard Library to find a huge floral arrangement of red roses in the shape of a cross. He and his classmates gaped at this extravagant display. Christy made no comment until, finally, several of them queried him, "What's this all about?"

Somewhat reluctantly, he admitted that each semester he too made a commitment to share Christ with ten people on Boston's North Shore. He had gone into a local florist's shop the day before to purchase flowers. While there, he led the proprietor to Christ. The florist brought the arrangement to campus, found out where Professor Wilson would be lecturing on evangelism, and placed the roses in front of the lectern in gratitude to the one who had shown him how to give his heart to Christ.[2]

Towards the end of his time at Gordon-Conwell, while Christy served as dean of the chapel, more than a hundred students signed a petition to invite John Wimber to campus as a guest speaker. This occurred at the peak of a controversy at Fuller Theological Seminary over a Signs and Wonders course taught by Wimber and church growth specialist C. Peter Wagner. During the summer of 1989, Christy and Betty decided to investigate on their own. They traveled to Long Island to attend a Wimber conference, seeking to test the spirits to see whether they were indeed of God (1 John 4:1). The conference generated so much interest that all 1,600 seats in the church were filled, and many people had to be turned away.

Sensing that the healings and words of knowledge were indeed a true work of God, Christy spoke with Wimber about the possibility of visiting Gordon-Conwell. A date was set for July 1991 to coincide with the annual Seminar on the Holy Spirit in World Evangelization. However, there were still those who opposed the visit of such a controversial figure, some because they were skeptical of such signs and wonders and some out of fear that trouble would erupt as it had at Fuller. Finally, everyone agreed that Wimber would speak at Gordon-Conwell for two days and then hold a practical demonstration of ministry at a nearby college on the third day, sponsored by the local Vineyard churches.

When the day of the practical demonstration arrived, over 1,200 people showed up—some skeptical, some seeking healing, some simply curious. During the service, several people were healed of long-term ailments, including friends of Christy. At one point, Wimber asked everyone to pray silently for the things they wanted God to do for them and through them. Christy prayed that the Lord would use him to reach Muslims with signs and wonders.

---

2.   Wayne Morgan, "Dr. J. Christy Wilson, Jr.—God's Tentmaker," (unpublished article), February 1999.

After the meeting, Christy sought out Wimber to express his gratitude. Wimber's closing words to Christy were, "Christy, while you were praying, the Lord showed me that you were asking him to work through you with signs and wonders among the Muslims. He wants you to know that he is going to do this through you!" For Christy, that was the highlight of the entire seminar.

During his tenure at Gordon-Conwell, it was mandatory that professors retire at age seventy. For Christy, as well as for his dear friend Gwyn Walters, that came in 1992, despite both of them feeling that they were still in their prime. Professor Wilson packed up his belongings and many of his books and files and, with his wife, set out for the next phase of their life's journey and ministry. Some who followed in his footsteps at Gordon-Conwell were surprised to find that, for one so well-groomed and neatly dressed, his office and files were a jumble of confusion.

After his retirement, Christy remained quite concerned about finding a replacement for himself at Gordon-Conwell. A former student, Tim Tennent, had since earned his PhD at Christy's alma mater, the University of Edinburgh, and had gained teaching experience at Toccoa Falls College in Georgia. Tim's wife, Julie, also graduated from Gordon-Conwell, and they were both close with Christy and Betty. Christy received a vision from God: "Tim Tennent will be the professor to take your place."

Professor Wilson at a Gordon-Conwell graduation ceremony
Courtesy of the Wilson family

The administration at Gordon-Conwell interviewed Tennent, but he felt conflicted. He loved Gordon-Conwell, but he was also quite happy where he was. He called Christy to seek his advice.

"I'm really torn," Tennent told his mentor.

Christy responded, "Tim, do you know what *alma mater* means?"

"Sure," Tennent replied, "it means *nourishing mother*."

"And when your mother calls, what do you do?" Christy asked. "And besides, we gave you Julie! You owe us a lot."

Tennent packed up and moved to Gordon-Conwell, where he taught until 2009.

Meanwhile, Christy and Betty settled into a new community in Duarte, California, to transition into retirement. Yet these years were to be among the most productive and challenging of their lives. Reflecting on the Gordon-Conwell season of his life with gratitude, Christy affectionately observed that those years were like "ice cream on the cake."

CHAPTER 16
DISCIPLINES FOR SPIRITUAL GROWTH

"Yes, I am the vine; you are the branches. Those who remain in me, and I in them, will produce much fruit. For apart from me you can do nothing."
John 15:5

In the margin of his Bible, Christy had written the following words near the beginning of John 15: "Fruit bearing by abiding, memorizing, praying."

He had also underlined the words of Philippians 1:6: "And I am certain that God, who began the good work within you, will continue his work until it is finally finished on the day when Christ Jesus returns."

Christy understood that spiritual growth is the result of God's work. Just as a seed does not do anything to make itself grow, so it is with spiritual growth within the child of God. It is the work of a loving, faithful, and sovereign God.

However, just as the presence of fertile soil, plentiful water, and bright sunlight greatly facilitates the growth of a tiny seedling into a mighty tree, there are also spiritual disciplines that can greatly facilitate the growth of a Christ-follower into a mighty man or woman of God.

An unknown writer once penned the following words of warning:

> Watch your thoughts, they become words.
> Watch your words, they become actions.
> Watch your actions, they become habits.

Watch your habits, they become your character.
Watch your character, it becomes your destiny.

The day-to-day actions and consistent habits in Christy's life clearly led to the fortitude of his character and destiny. His most prominent practices included Bible reading, Scripture memorization, personal evangelism, and prayer.

A foundational discipline in Christy's life was Bible reading. Through the nurture of his parents—primarily his father—he quickly came to love the Bible. During his childhood in Persia, he learned the Bible through family devotions each morning, and he was soon devouring its adventurous stories and wisdom on his own.

As a high school student, his teachers taught him higher criticism, a secular approach to the Bible that is speculative by nature and based primarily on reason rather than revelation. Christy faced a theological fork in the road and had an important choice to make; however, it proved to be an easy decision for him:

> At first I believed these theories because I thought the teachers knew more about these things than I did. Yet through my habit of reading the Bible each day—which my father encouraged—I realized that these critical views did not agree with the original Source.
>
> When I began to investigate all the attacks on Scripture, I found that the Bible was right in every single case. So by investigation and by faith, I accepted the Scriptures as the infallible Word of God. Since then, I have turned to the Scriptures when anyone has come to me with a problem and have found the solution there each time.
>
> If it is the Word of God and so is without error, we don't have to be afraid of investigation. It has been wonderful to see how God has honored His Word and shown it to be absolutely dependable.

Throughout their adult years, Christy and Betty arose early each morning and began the day together with Bible reading, Scripture memorization, and prayer. "You usually don't have people knocking at your door at five o'clock in the morning unless there's an emergency. Therefore, we would do our praying and our study of the Scripture and our memorizing at that time. Also, I find that reading over verses before going to bed helps a lot because your subconscious mind deals with them."

Christy established the personal discipline of reading through the entire Bible each year, using a different translation each time. The New Living Translation (NLT) emerged as his favorite, but he also enjoyed the New International Version and the King James. His Bibles, especially his NLT TouchPoint Bible, were full of markings—key passages underlined and fresh insights scribbled in the margins.

With each rereading Christy would also study a different theme. One year he concentrated on God's promises, marking each one he encountered, and when December 31 rolled around, he had found over thirty thousand promises in Scripture. Christy remained a lifelong student and lover of the word of God.

A second discipline was Scripture memorization. One of his annual study themes was to select a key verse from every chapter of the Bible and begin hiding it in his heart. "By memorizing the key verse of every chapter, you can get the key verses of every book—1,100 verses. Then you have a wonderful way to get the context. When you learn a verse, you know what is around it, and that way you can master the Bible. I'm calling this 'Stepping Stones through the Scriptures,' because each key verse of each chapter is a stepping stone as you go through the Scriptures."

He assembled these key verses well before the age of the copier or personal computer, so he had to type out all 1,100 on a typewriter, using carbon paper to make "Stepping Stones through the Scriptures" available to each of his children. When he suggested that they memorize every verse, he was met with smirks and eye rolls. However, in their adult years his children gratefully took up the challenge.

Christy got started in Scripture memorization through the influence of two great ministry pioneers—Stacey Woods, founder of InterVarsity/USA, and Dawson Trotman, founder of The Navigators. Stacey invited Dawson to come to an InterVarsity staff conference in Canada, and Dawson accepted the invitation—but with one condition: everyone on the staff, including Stacey, had to sign up for the Topical Memory System. This introductory, ordered approach to Scripture memorization proved to be a tremendous experience for Christy, and he made his way through the whole set of sixty verses. Dawson also taught him that the secret to retaining the memory verses within his heart and mind was repetition.

One of the many ways that memorizing Scripture benefited Christy's life was in resisting temptation. Referring to Jesus' encounter with the devil in the wilderness, he observed that "if Christ had had to get a Bible and look up a reference, he wouldn't have had time. Or if he'd said, 'Well, I think it says something about that somewhere . . . ,' it would not have had the same power. Jesus knew it, by heart. He therefore quoted and overcame the temptation."

Christy also found Scripture memorization useful in deliverance ministry. "When someone is oppressed with demons, the demons will have to listen to Scripture." He observed that when you confront demons with Scripture, such as Revelation 12:11 or 1 John 4:4, and order them out in the name of Christ, it has amazing power.

Evangelism was another area where Christy benefited from his memorization of Scripture. "If you don't have the Scriptures with you, and you're in a conversation with someone on the airplane, or wherever, the Holy Spirit, if you have verses in your heart, can bring them to mind, and I'm even sometimes amazed because it's something I haven't even thought of. The Holy Spirit reveals a truth right on the spot through his Word. That's why it's so important to know the Scriptures in order to lead people to Christ and also in order to be able to disciple them."

This observation highlights a third spiritual discipline in Christy's life—personal evangelism. Christy was a lifelong evangelist, and few people had an evangelistic spirit like he had. His witness was founded on his bedrock convictions that people needed the Lord and were spiritually lost without him, that the Lord Jesus Christ gave us the assignment of bringing the good news to the world, and that the Holy Spirit empowers us to be his witnesses. Evangelism was for him both a privilege and a responsibility.

Christy was solidly convinced of the gospel and never relinquished that conviction. During the first few weeks of his seminary classes, he usually taught about the lostness of humanity and the necessity of Christ's atoning death for us. Someone would invariably raise their hand with the question, "Dr. Wilson, are you actually saying that if someone does not receive Jesus as their Savior and Lord, they will be eternally separated from God?" And his answer was always the same: "Absolutely that's what I'm saying." He believed the bad news of our spiritual bankruptcy and utter lostness, and he believed that it is this bad news that makes the good news of salvation so wonderful and so worth sharing with anyone and everyone. He never lost his urgency in sharing the gospel, and there was never any hint of doubt in him about the veracity of the gospel message.

He witnessed when he ate at restaurants, getting to know the waitresses and leaving a small gospel tract to accompany his generous tips.

He witnessed during a weeklong vacation at a dude ranch in Wyoming, befriending the entire staff and sharing the gospel with them so passionately that they sobbed when he left.

He witnessed when he wrote letters. In a letter to the founder of McDonald's regarding a nutritional issue, he included a simple gospel presentation just in case Ray Kroc had not yet heard this good news.

Though it was risky, he witnessed to the four Afghans who served as helpers in the Wilsons' Kabul home by leading an evangelistic Bible study for them in their own language.

He witnessed whenever he traveled by airplane for speaking engagements. In fact, he made it a personal policy never to sit next to other Christians who might be traveling with him—for doing so would deny him the opportunity to witness to whoever the airlines had assigned to sit next to him. During one flight, he had already shared the gospel with the person on his left during takeoff and the person on his right while the plane was ascending. When the plane reached its cruising altitude, Christy was up on his knees, turned around in his seat to share the gospel with the people behind him.

Christy would often start by striking up conversations with strangers, asking them about themselves. "Where are you flying to?" "Where are you from?" Invariably they would ask him the reason he was traveling, and it was usually for some gospel purpose. Before they knew it, he was sharing the gospel with them in a natural and winsome manner.[1]

Above all else, Christy was a man of prayer. While his father built into him an insatiable hunger for God's word, his mother nurtured within his heart a love for prayer. Her influence in this area was so strong that, after Christy Sr. died, Christy called his mother almost every evening to share specific prayer needs.

However, to call prayer a discipline in Christy's life is not entirely accurate. Prayer for him was a joy, like the joy a songbird finds in singing. It was a privilege, just as an Olympic athlete is privileged to represent his country. It was a compulsion, the way your lungs are compelled to suck in oxygen. Prayer was the hallmark of his life.

Christy kept an extensive journal of private prayers that he would revisit each day. On its pages were the names of many, many people for whom he interceded, and he usually included a verse for each one.

---

1. Tim Tennent witnessed this scene as he sat two aisles over and one row back from Christy on an airplane.

Excerpt from Christy Wilson's 1953 prayer journal
Courtesy of Archives of the Billy Graham Center, Wheaton, IL

As mentioned in a previous chapter, Christy would pray before he drove anywhere—a habit his children and grandchildren continue to this day. A reporter for the *Manchester Guardian* once accompanied Christy on a drive in Afghanistan. In his write-up of the experience, the journalist observed that Christy prayed before he drove. He also noted that, though himself an atheist, he too began to pray for Christy's driving!

A colleague at Gordon-Conwell reflected that he only saw Christy get angry once during his entire eighteen-year ministry there. One year, the print shop at Gordon-Conwell was delayed in producing the annual community directory, and it would not be available until Christmas time. Most people were slightly annoyed because they could not look up a classmate's phone number or match a particular face with a name. Christy, however, was terribly upset about this delay. It was impeding his prayer life; it was delaying his prayer book. "There are hundreds of students," he protested, "who are not being prayed for!"

In evangelism, Christy found prayer to be an effective means of opening hearts to the gospel, as one occasion in Afghanistan illustrates:

> An Afghan friend came to me with his uncle who needed a cataract operation. They had just been turned away from the government hospital where

they were told that a bed for him to have the operation would not be available for three months.

My friend explained to me that this made it very difficult since his uncle came from the central highlands which was a journey of several days each way. It therefore would be difficult for him to make the trip and come back in three months. On the other hand it would be very hard for him to stay in Kabul, the capital, away from his family for three months. He asked me whether I knew the head of that government hospital. I said that I did. He then asked me kindly to write a note explaining the situation and asking whether it might not be possible to admit his uncle sooner. I replied that I did not have to write a note but would personally speak to the head of the hospital.

The friend then asked me what the name was of the one in charge of the hospital. I answered, "His name is the Lord Jesus Christ. He is the Head of every hospital." I then said, "Let us talk to Him now." Praying in their language, I explained the situation to the Lord and asked Him to help. I then told them to go back to the government hospital. But they were reluctant to return there since they had just been turned away. I said to them, "You asked me to intercede with the Head of the hospital and I did this. Now go back." Finally they agreed to try again.

Several hours later my friend returned to see me and he was all excited. He exclaimed, "You do know the Head of that hospital!" He went on to explain that as soon as they returned, a patient was just being discharged and they admitted his uncle immediately, putting him in the bed which had just been vacated. And they would perform the needed operation soon. This man became a believer in Jesus Christ as his personal Lord and Savior.

• • •

The disciplines in Christy's life were not something that he laboriously mustered up, nor did he plod through them with a grimaced face. They were the joyful byproduct of a life in the Spirit. They resonated from a soul that was in tune with God.

Christy was constantly inviting the Lord to fill him more. On August 1, 1968, during a brief furlough in New Jersey, he took out a blank piece of paper and wrote a prayer of surrender and consecration to the Holy Spirit:

> Dear Holy Spirit of God,
>
> I sign my life away to Thee asking that Thou will control all the rest of my life, that Thou will fill me constantly with Thyself, that the Father's will may be done through me, that you will minister any gifts of your choosing through me, that you will help me overcome temptations through the death of Jesus Christ for me on the cross, that you will overcome Satan through me by the power of Jesus' blood, that you will glorify the Lord Jesus through me, that you will bear your full fruit in my life and that many who are lost may find salvation through me and others, that we may see great revivals, that Christians may be built up and constantly love one another, that the Church may be purged and cleansed and no longer be a reproach to God in the world, that I may have utterance and boldness and that Christ's commission may be completed in this generation.
>
> In Jesus' glorious name,
> J. Christy Wilson Jr.

Seeking to remain filled with the Spirit continually, Christy repeated a simple petition from his prayer journal almost every day:

> Dear Lord, I pray for
>
> The power of Your Holy Spirit in witnessing
>
> The utterance of Your Holy Spirit in speaking
>
> The wisdom of Your Holy Spirit in researching
>
> The unction of Your Holy Spirit in preaching
>
> The graciousness of Your Holy Spirit in relating
>
> The intercession of Your Holy Spirit in praying
>
> The direction (guidance) of Your Holy Spirit in deciding
>
> The understanding of Your Holy Spirit in studying
>
> The understanding of Your Holy Spirit in reading
>
> The protection of Your Holy Spirit in living
>
> The knowledge of Your Holy Spirit in teaching
>
> The vision of Your Holy Spirit in strategizing
>
> The love of Your Holy Spirit in serving
>
> The remembrance of Your Holy Spirit in fulfilling
>
> The efficiency of Your Holy Spirit in working

These prayers are a window into how deeply Christy relied on the Holy Spirit both for daily living and for any enduring fruit that his life might bear. As he entered his challenging final years, with sickness overtaking his body, the habits he had cultivated for so long kept him close to the Lord.

CHAPTER 17
THE SUNSET YEARS

*My health may fail, and my spirit may grow weak, but God
remains the strength of my heart; he is mine forever.*
Psalm 73:26

Before retiring from Gordon-Conwell, Christy traveled to Indianapolis to attend the Congress on the Holy Spirit and World Evangelization. During his time there, a doctor and his wife who had just returned from Kabul delivered a letter to Christy. Within it was a personal invitation to visit Afghanistan. "Lord, what is your will?" Christy had been praying.

During one of the sessions, a man who Christy had never met before, Paul Cain, was speaking. Cain, who had the gift of prophecy, suddenly stopped short and pointed directly at him, saying, "Christy Wilson, God is going to take you back to Afghanistan, and you will be accepted by the people who once rejected you."

That prophecy was fulfilled in 1991 when Christy and Betty returned to Kabul for three weeks to work and pray among the followers of Christ in Afghanistan. They attended a Christian Workers' Conference, met with Gordon-Conwell alumni who were serving in Kabul, and worshiped on Easter morning with CCCK.

During the Easter sunrise service, as worshipers sang "Because He Lives" with great gusto, scud missiles roared overhead. The battle for Khost was being waged a hundred miles south of Kabul, and hundreds of scuds were being launched from the capital while the *mujahideen* were firing rockets into the city.

During their time in Kabul the American embassy was closed, as were the British, German, Japanese, and many other embassies. Only the Indian embassy remained open besides the Russian embassy and those of other Communist nations. It was a difficult trip for Christy and Betty, partly because of the sadness of having to leave Gordon-Conwell before they were fully prepared to and partly because they encountered so many changes within the country they had been forced to leave eighteen years earlier.

Not long after they returned from Kabul they moved into Westminster Gardens, the retirement community in Duarte, California, where Christy's parents had lived.

"We shouldn't be here," Betty observed. "These people are too old!"

"Well, Betty, we're getting old too!" Christy replied warmly.

Among the friends they made at Westminster Gardens was a group of ten to fifteen Princeton alumni who gathered on the second Saturday morning of each month. The Prayer for Princeton group, as they called themselves, would enjoy lunch together, reminisce about their Princeton years, and sometimes sing favorite songs.

Prayer for Princeton group (Christy, standing third
from left, and Betty, standing far right) and banner
Courtesy of Bill Grady (Princeton '51)

But most of all, they prayed together. They prayed from specific Bible passages that God would restore to Princeton its Christian heritage, spiritual values, and moral commitment. Each year, two or three members journeyed to New Jersey for the annual Princeton reunion. While there, they would pray with other alumni each evening in the Faculty Room of Nassau Hall from seven o'clock until midnight.[1]

During the fiftieth reunion, Christy gave each classmate who was present a copy of his book *More to Be Desired Than Gold*. This book, compiled by a Gordon-Conwell student for Christy's seventieth birthday, was filled with stories that Christy had told countless times about what God had done through his people around the world. Christy inscribed within each book a personal invitation to accept the Lord. Twenty-five years earlier, soon after a classmate had died, Christy had written individual letters to each of his classmates inviting them to come to the eternal reunion in heaven. He found that, when witnessing with affection, understanding, and concern, people were very responsive. And like Paul, Christy did not want to be found guilty of anyone's blood (Acts 20:26–27).

During his trips to Princeton, Christy often spoke and led worship services at local churches. He rarely spoke anywhere without making it very clear how to receive the Lord.

While there, Christy would stay with Burnett and Dorothy Sams, close friends since the 1970s. In 1975 he played a pivotal role in helping them open the Lamplighter, a Christian bookstore at 240 Nassau Street. Christy had encouraged them in the business venture, asserting with great certainty, "This is of God!" He also encouraged them with his billfold. Although Christy could not realistically afford to give money, he was always willing and blessed to do so.

"This is seed money to get that bookstore started," Christy told Burnett as he gave the first donation. And as Burnett received it from Christy's hand, he thought to himself, *If we accept this check, then we are committed to raise the rest of the money and to move forward with opening the bookstore.* And that he did. All along the way, Christy offered guidance by sharing a wealth of knowledge about bookstores.

---

1. Van Wallach, "Praying for Princeton's Soul," *Princeton Alumni Weekly Magazine,* May 20, 1998; and Abby Love Smith, "Life in Nassau Hall," *Christian Observer Magazine,* July 2006.

The Lamplighter opened in September 1975 and remained in service until 2002, when it finally closed its doors. The building was donated to Christian Union, a ministry to all eight Ivy League schools, and subsequently transformed into the Wilson Center, devoted to Christian ministry, literature, and hospitality. The plaque in the entryway to the Wilson Center is engraved with the following words:

THE J. CHRISTY WILSON, JR. CENTER

J. Christy Wilson, Jr. was born of missionary parents in Tabriz, Iran, graduated from Princeton University in 1944 and subsequently Princeton Theological Seminary. He took his Ph.D. at the University of Edinburgh in Scotland. He was Missionary Secretary for InterVarsity at the time of the first student convention in Toronto, Canada in 1946 (which was later moved to Urbana, IL). He and his wife Betty went to Afghanistan in 1951 as tentmakers, teaching for twenty-two years. In 1974, he became Professor of World Evangelization at Gordon-Conwell Theological Seminary and went to be with our Lord on February 8, 1999. Because of his many years of service for the Christian well-being of the Princeton community, this building is dedicated as a Christian ministry center in his name.

In addition to his trips to Princeton, Christy frequently received requests to teach and speak at conferences around America. One such invitation came from Montreat-Anderson College in North Carolina; Christy was asked to deliver the Staley Lectures on missions. Billy and Ruth Graham lived near the college, and Ruth did much to encourage the students and promote interest in missions. While Christy was in Montreat, Ruth attended his lectures. One evening she invited him to their rustic mountaintop home, where he warmed himself by the "laughing fire" Ruth often described in her books and admired a beautiful painting of Billy. Ruth sent someone to pick up several buckets of Kentucky Fried Chicken, and she and Christy began to talk.

Since Billy was away at the time, Ruth asked Christy to write down for him a story he had told in one of his lectures. Billy liked it and later used it as an illustration in a message:

> One time I was on an airplane in Afghanistan, preparing for departure. The door was shut, our seat belts were fastened, and we thought we were ready for take-off. Suddenly, through the window, I saw a man running toward the plane. I thought he must be one of the passengers who was late and wondered whether they would let him on. Sure enough, he started pounding on the door of the plane.
>
> The flight attendant looked at his watch. It was time for us to leave, so he was not about to open the door. But the man kept pounding louder and louder. Finally the flight attendant went back and opened the door a crack to see who it was. There, to everyone's amazement, stood the pilot!
>
> We had locked the pilot out of the plane!
>
> The ramp had already been pulled away, so they had to grab him by the elbows and hoist him up into the plane. As the pilot walked up the aisle, the Afghans—who have a good sense of humor— roared with laughter. He then got into the cockpit, and we took off.
>
> When this happened, I thought how much our lives are like this. We think we are in the right place and are all set to take off for heaven. But the question is, "Have we left the Pilot out?"
>
> Jesus said, "Behold, I stand at the door and knock. If anyone hears My voice and opens the door, I will come in." He not only comes in to save us from our sins, but He has the flight plan for our

lives which guides our ministry and ultimately takes us to heaven.

This was but one of many stories that Christy loved to share, and it was among the stories he told most frequently. His storytelling was usually sprinkled with warm chuckles and a wide, boyish grin.

On December 27, 1996, he included this same story about the locked-out pilot when he addressed the twenty thousand people assembled for Urbana. Commemorating the fiftieth anniversary of the first InterVarsity missions conference, Dan Harrison, the director of Urbana '96, introduced Christy Wilson, the director of the first conference. Christy addressed the participants for only seven minutes, but he weaved in stories about his childhood in Iran, the first missions conference fifty years earlier, tentmaking ministry in Afghanistan, and lives changed by the power of God.

Christy speaking at the Urbana missions conference in 1996
Courtesy of the Wilson family

In the same year Christy journeyed to Rome with Jim Cudney and James Ritchey to meet with the exiled king of Afghanistan, Mohammed Zahir Shah, whose son Christy had tutored forty-four years earlier in Kabul. The purpose of their meeting was to propose a *loya jirga*, a traditional Afghan assembly convened for solving major problems in which the assembled group appoints an elder and everyone agrees to abide by his ruling. The purpose of this *loya jirga* would be to seek restoration and peace between the warring factions in Afghanistan.

The trip came about through a friendship between Mr. Cudney and Shah Mahmud Ghazi, the cousin and brother-in-law of the king. Together they developed a plan for reconstruction through a Joint International Reconstruction Group for Afghanistan (JIRGA). The plan called for the exiled king to head up the JIRGA and try to bring peace, security, and stability to the country he had ruled for forty years. The period of his reign is remembered by many as "the golden years" for the Afghan people, years of peace and prosperity when, instead of suffering hunger, Afghans exported food. The king desired to return to his native land, not as king, but to broker a peace settlement, and he made a definite decision to return.

The Americans met with the king for two hours and twenty minutes, during which time they were warmly received. They were then escorted to the king's residence by Prince Mustapha Zahir, where they met with Mustapha and General Sardar Abdul Wali for the rest of the day and again for most of another. Mustapha was a favorite grandson of the king; he

Christy with Mohammed Zahir Shah (center) and grandson Mustapha Zahir in Rome
Courtesy of the Wilson family

served as his eyes and ears, had an impressive grasp of the Afghan situation, and was candid during their discussions.

During their time with the king and his grandson, the team discussed several historical events in Afghanistan, including the destruction of the church, the establishment of an eye hospital, and ongoing work with the blind. They also presented the king with an album of pictures taken during his rule, Christy's book *One Hundred Afghan Persian Proverbs*, and the JESUS film in Dari. In all, they spent thirteen hours consulting with these Afghan leaders and friends.[2]

The Taliban and the other groups invited to the *loya jirga* accepted the exiled king as their chosen elder. However, unknown to everyone at that time, Christy's life was soon to take a major

---

2. Internationals Serving Asians, annual meeting minutes, August 2, 1997, Hephzibah Heights, Monterey, MA.

turn, and the *loya jirga* of all the parties never occurred. (Some have speculated that had it happened, there might have been no place for Osama bin Laden in Afghanistan, and perhaps September 11, 2001, would have turned out differently.)

Several years later Mohammed Zahir Shah sent a letter to Christy on official letterhead:

THE OFFICE OF HIS MAJESTY,
THE FORMER KING OF AFGHANISTAN

Rome, December 12, 1998

Dear Dr. Wilson,

It was with great pleasure that I received your letter of December 10, 1998. Thank you very much indeed for your kind words and warm sentiments.

I regret very much to hear of your illness. I pray to Almighty God to restore your health once again. The Almighty God always looks after those who do good deeds and you have done many good deeds both in Afghanistan and elsewhere. With love and caring you have touched the lives of many people who needed it the most, such as blind people.

In closing my letter, I once again thank you for your kind letter and pray to Almighty God to shine His Light upon the brave Afghan Nation and to restore freedom, peace, dignity and honor to our people.

With Best Wishes,
Mohammad Zaher

The illness to which the exiled king referred first made its presence known during a trip Christy had taken to Turkey to speak to a group of missionaries in the spring. He felt weak and fainted as he walked back to his accommodations after speaking. Later that year, at a conference in Northern California, he again felt weak and began to cough uncontrollably. Due to his busy work schedule, Christy remained quite tired, and what appeared to be symptoms of a cold or pneumonia lingered without improvement. He and Betty were staying in a friend's home when a terrible coughing fit came upon him, and he simply couldn't catch his breath.

Shortly after that, in August, he and Betty flew together to Colorado Springs for a Kabul reunion. When they arrived at their destination, Christy immediately went to bed. John Hankins, a doctor who was also at the reunion, suspected that Christy's health problems were far more serious than a cold or pneumonia. That night Christy experienced another terrible coughing spell, making him fall out of bed and faint.

The following morning Dr. Hankins had him admitted to the hospital for X-rays, but liquid in his lungs prevented an accurate reading. Christy spoke again that evening and then collapsed onto his bed.

The next day, he returned home to Duarte and immediately went to see his personal physician, Dr. Walton. X-rays were once again inconclusive due to excessive fluid in his lungs, which were barely visible on the film, and Christy could still hardly breathe. While a lung specialist drained the fluid from his lungs, Christy sat at a table with a tube in his chest, at the other end of which was a huge bag rapidly filling.

The following morning, a CAT scan revealed a cancerous mass between the two lobes of his lungs. Extensive surgery at the University of Southern California Teaching Hospital was unable to remove the tumor, so the doctor encased it to prevent additional fluid. The form of cancer that was growing within Christy's body attacked the nerve endings in his chest wall. He needed more and more oxygen and was forced to inhale it through an oxygen mask, which he came to loathe.

A short time later, many weeks of chemotherapy commenced for Christy. He stayed home as much as possible, and Cleo Shook, his friend from Afghanistan, accompanied him for his infusions of chemo. Through it all, Christy made every attempt to carry on life as naturally as possible.

One Sunday afternoon he complained, "I'm really having trouble breathing." His doctor instructed him to go immediately to the emergency room, where they gave him oxygen and tried to make him comfortable. But he was very ill at ease in the hospital, and Betty regretted that she didn't bring him right back home again.

Christy and Betty in 1997, shortly before his final illness
Courtesy of the Wilson family

They tried to make his hospital room as homey as possible. Nancy was in California to be with her father, and she stayed with him until five o'clock in the morning. He was later transferred to the nursing home at Westminster Gardens and eventually brought home, where he was much happier. A five-hundred-gallon oxygen tank dominated their porch, though, and soon, when he needed the maximum amount of oxygen possible, even larger tanks of frozen oxygen were provided, each one lasting about a week. A myriad of tubes meandered from the tanks into the bedroom, and a mask covered Christy's face.

Many people visited Christy during his final illness, including longtime friends and others who simply desired to pray and lay hands on him. When he was feeling well, he was grateful to see them. When he felt weak from labored breathing, however, he grew weary of continual visitors.

Some told him, "Christy, if you have faith, God will heal you."

But Christy's reply was, "The question isn't if I have faith; it's what is God's will."

He eventually concluded, "If the Lord wants to heal me, he can. But we don't need to continually have so many people here." It became evident that some boundaries needed to be established, and a sign stating "No Visitors" was placed on his door.

One very close friend from Christy's Princeton days, Bill Antablan, also lived in Westminster Gardens with his wife, and he visited Christy regularly and graciously. He would simply read a short passage of Scripture to Christy and pray with him and then leave. Christy was greatly encouraged by his visits.

Doug Birdsall flew in from Japan, and Tim Tennent arrived from Massachusetts. These former students also spent time with Christy and were a source of comfort to him.

During the Christmas season, Christy was so tired of the mask that he suggested, "Why don't we just take it off and let the Lord take me?"

But Chris urged his father, "We want you to be with us for a while longer!"

During Christy's final days in the early weeks of the new year, his family surrounded him, and an eighty-seven-year-old missionary nurse, Trudy Winkleman, offered them help. She would quietly come each day, pick up the laundry and bedding, wash it, and bring it back, leaving it neatly folded on the front porch. Another nurse gave Christy medication to calm him, but he was terrified of taking it after the first time since it affected his thinking. Eventually, however, it would prove to be helpful to him.

During his final weeks Chris and Nancy, both of whom lived on the East Coast, took turns being with their parents, and Marty, who lived in the area, tried to be there as much as possible. When Christy's weakness left him totally bound to his bed, he would move his arms and legs and gesture for one of them to bring him his prayer list. He prayed over that list again and again.

A few days before Christy died, Marty was visiting, but he was assigned to travel to a conference on the East Coast with his new company. Christy exhorted him, "Marty, you must go!" Reluctantly, Marty said a special goodbye to his father and flew back east.

During his final thirty-six hours Christy began lapsing into unconsciousness, and Betty and Nancy sat by his bed. At one point, when Christy began to stir, Nancy spoke softly into his ear, "Dad, I love you." His reply, "I love you too," would be his last words. He died peacefully at home on Monday, February 8, 1999. Betty and Nancy were with him, and just a few minutes before he died, Trudy was able to join them. Chris had recently returned to his home in Florida and Marty was traveling, but both immediately flew back to California for the funeral and memorial service preparations.

A memorial service was held on February 13 at First Presbyterian Church in the neighboring city of Monrovia, and another was held at Gordon-Conwell on March 5.

J. Christy Wilson Jr. was buried in Duarte next to the gravesite of his father and mother. On his gravestone are the words, "And so shall we ever be with the Lord" (1 Thessalonians 4:17).

CHAPTER 18
REFLECTIONS

*But my life is worth nothing to me unless I use it for finishing
the work assigned me by the Lord Jesus—the work of telling
others the Good News about the wonderful grace of God.*
Acts 20:24

There are many different things for which a person can exchange their life. Some will endure and others will not. A list of those things that will not endure is quite long: riches, fame, strength, knowledge, possessions, power, status, our physical bodies, kingdoms, nations, the heavens, the earth. However, that which endures forever is a short list indeed: God, God's word, human souls, and love (Psalm 90:2; 1 Peter 1:23–25; 1 John 5:11–13; 1 Corinthians 13:8).

Christy Wilson invested his life in the latter.

He was certainly not perfect, and he made no pretense to be. Like all of us, he had his flaws and foibles, his troubles and trials. But he followed hard after his Lord Jesus Christ.

In a farewell address to Christy and Betty on the day before they departed Afghanistan, one of the church elders remarked,

> We all knew of Christy before we ever met him! . . .
> I first heard of him when an Archbishop, no less—
> though then a bishop—was paying a visit here. He
> was on his way to the Anglican Lambeth Confer-
> ence in 1958. I asked him why he should be going
> via Kabul; he said, "To meet Dr. Wilson."

Christy has walked with kings, archbishops, and world leaders, nor lost the common touch. To know Dr. Wilson is to have an open door into many places here in this city and world-wide. An Afghan said to [my wife] this week that he had never met a kinder man than Christy and that his courtesy and kindness were seen in his face.

Cathie Shook Ritchey, who was a rambunctious ten-year-old when Christy first served as her pastor in Kabul, reflected,

Christy became a friend and mentor as well as my pastor. As busy as he seemed to be, he always had time to talk when any of us needed him—adults or we children and teens.

Those of us young people who studied under him for church membership caught more about prayer than we were taught about prayer. His example was lived right there in front of us. There was no hypocrisy in him. He lived everything he believed. And Uncle Christy was the most humble man I have ever known.

During a Sunday school lesson I was teaching a few years ago, one of the questions for the class was, "Of all the Christians you have known, tell us about the one who reminded you the most of the Lord Jesus." As the teacher I was able to wrap up the class with some stories of Uncle Christy. Honestly, I have not known another person whom I respected more than I did him.

One thing I can say about the young couples who served in Kabul, many of them named their children after Uncle Christy. Both girls and boys received his name. If I remember correctly, there were five families who were at the memorial service for Uncle Christy, who had children carrying his name.

Christy Wilson during his seminary professor days
Courtesy of the Wilson family

Christy's secretary at Gordon-Conwell, Holly Greening, said of him,

> The thing I remember most is what a caring, giving person he was. Every time he would come to my office, he would walk in the door and ask me how I was, and not just a generic asking, but a real wanting to know what was going on in your life. Before he'd leave my office, he'd always say a prayer for me.
>
> Out of all the people I've ever known, I would have to say that Christy Wilson most exemplifies our idea of how Jesus would relate with people. He had a "glow" about him—the presence of the Holy Spirit in his life was evident not just in his inner appearance but also in his outward physical appearance. He was an honest, humble, prayerful, caring, giving, kind, warm, godly person. I never saw him angry and never heard him say anything unkind. To this day, I seek to be as good an example of how a Christian should act to those with whom they

come in contact. I pray that one day I may reach that goal.

His student, mentee, and the president of Asbury Theological Seminary, Tim Tennent, noted, "For those of us who knew Christy Wilson, he was the best example of godly radiance, of zeal, of passion, of vibrancy. There were no 'standing puddles' in the recesses of his heart—no, it was always an overflowing stream.

"No one had an evangelistic spirit like he had. He was a leader in thinking through new mission strategy and a pioneer in the area of tentmaking. He had a wonderful way of blending together personal testimony and strategy."

His good friends during the last several decades of his life, Dorothy and Burnett Sams, observed that "he was very careful how he spent life's moments. During his visits with us, when 9:00 in the evening rolled around, he would say, 'Oh, I have to go to bed,' and then he would spend some time with the Lord. Then at 4:00 the next morning, he had his light on and he was talking with the Lord. Christy valued time, every minute. He made good use of his time, and he didn't wallow away his time."

Wendy Murray Zoba, Christy's student and a former associate editor for *Christianity Today*, noted in a tribute to his life, "Christy Wilson was my standard for what it meant to be a Christian. . . . He has left a legacy of people, like me, whose lives have been moved to a new place (often literally) through knowing him. And he has left us a picture of what it means to be a lover of Christ."[1]

Mark Dever, senior pastor of Capitol Hill Baptist Church in Washington, DC, described him in a sermon on prayer:

> A professor I had in seminary, Christy Wilson, would pray whenever you mentioned anything to him, right then and there. It didn't matter if you

---

1. Quoted in Michael Maudlin, "What Would J. Christy Wilson Do?," *Christianity Today*, April 5, 1999.

were on your way to take a final examination. If you'd see him in the hall and you just mentioned something—a concern—and asked him to pray about it, he would say, "Let's pray right now." And then he would stop whatever he was doing, and you would certainly stop whatever you were doing, bow your head right there with everybody walking by, and he would just start praying. And he did it in the most wonderful, focused way that glorified God, showing this immediate, joyful, childlike, constant trust in his heavenly Father.

After Mark had finished preaching this sermon, he was approached by Christy's adult granddaughter, who happened to be visiting that Sunday. "You described my grandfather exactly," she told him. "That's what he was always like. He always would just stop and pray."[2]

Robert Henderson, an author and retired pastor, reflected,

He did not have a dramatic personality in any sense of the word. Rather, he was a gentle, passionate advocate for missions. And he was a man who prayed. It was his prayers that took him soon thereafter to Afghanistan, where to be public as a Christian can cost you your life.

Christy "infected" his students with his priority on prayer in the work of mission. He had the students pray for all their classmates and draw a map of the world to learn where every nation was. He himself prayed daily for the student body of the seminary. He knew their names and the names of

---

2. "I Am Praying" (sermon), Capitol Hill Baptist Church, Washington, DC, May 5, 2013.

their family members. The sweet aroma of Christ was present, simply because he was there.

He was not intellectually "demanding." Only this: he communicated Christ's compassion for the world outside to his generations of students.[3]

Christy with Betty, their three children, their grandchildren, and his mother-in-law in 1987
Courtesy of the Wilson family

Christy's younger sister, Nancy Lang, noted, "To me, he's the best Christian I've ever met."

Billy Graham sent the following message to be read at Christy Wilson's memorial service at Gordon-Conwell on March 5, 1999:

> At this time of celebration of the life of Dr. Christy Wilson, Ruth and I want to join his family and many friends in giving thanks for this godly man. We praise God for the many gifts and talents He entrusted to Dr. Wilson. J. Christy Wilson will go down in history as one of the great and courageous missionaries for the gospel in the twentieth century. His many experiences in Afghanistan and other places will long be remembered. His sharing experiences and views concerning missions have made

---

3.   "The Gift of Christy Wilson," *reNEWS*, June 1999.

a great impact on Christian students, not only here in America but throughout the world. I thank God for his life and ministry. Though his loss will be keenly felt here, we rejoice in knowing that he is face to face with the Lord, whom he served so faithfully.

Billy

In addition to a memorial service for Christy, Gordon-Conwell also established the J. Christy Wilson Jr. Center for World Missions, and they dedicated a building on campus as the Wilson House. The old storage closet in which Christy started a world prayer meeting at noon each day was transformed into the Wilson Prayer Chapel.

• • •

Christy Wilson's passions were evangelism and missions. His life-blood was prayer. His character displayed kindness and love. And his countenance exuded vibrancy and joy.

When it came to the defining hallmarks of his life—intercessory prayer, personal evangelism, world missions, and God's word—he certainly believed in the importance of such things. He even taught these priceless treasures to a long procession of students. But he went beyond that.

He *did* them; he *lived* them.

He was an intercessor and a prayer warrior like few people before or after him.

He was compelled to share the good news of salvation in Christ with anyone and everyone he could, and he did so in a winsome, respectful, natural, and compelling manner.

He took the gospel to a nation of twelve million people when there were few known Christians among those twelve million, and he helped launch countless other Christ-followers to the ends of the earth as missionaries.

He devoured God's word on a daily basis, remaining a lifelong student of the Bible, and he continually hid large portions of it within his heart.

Christy Wilson left a lasting legacy. The ripple effect of his life continues to spread to people, ethnic groups, and nations throughout the world. His life continues to grow God's kingdom and to reveal the splendor of the God he loved so much and served so well.

ACKNOWLEDGMENTS

I am grateful for Christy Wilson's many ministry partners and colleagues, students and fellow professors, and friends and family who shared their stories and remembrances with me.

I especially wish to thank Christy's wife, Betty; his younger sister, Nancy Lang; his daughter, Nancy; and his sons, Chris and Marty, who graciously shared their time, memories, and stories with great generosity.

Many people provided valuable details, stories, and insights that breathed life into this biography, including Cully Anderson, Ivan S. Chow, Robert Cooley, Margaret Cudney, Jacque Friberg, Bob Golon, Bill Grady, Holly Greening, Albrecht Hauser, Libby Little, Kristy McNeil, Greg Parsons, Cathie Shook Ritchey, Burnett and Dorothy Sams, John Sanders, Tim Tennent, Mair Walters, David Wells, and Meghan Wisdom. In addition, Dudley Woodberry's introduction provided a valuable historical context for understanding Christy's life and ministry.

It has been my pleasure and delight to work alongside the wonderful people at William Carey Library. From inception to writing to editing to publication, their encouragement and expertise helped shape this book in many valuable ways.

Bob Shuster of the Billy Graham Center Archives in Wheaton, Illinois, spent many hours interviewing Christy when he was alive, and those transcripts provided priceless details. Katherine Graber graciously assisted me during my days of research at the Billy Graham Center Archives.

Special thanks to Gina Bolton, Sue Collier, and Mark Mlynarski, who reviewed the completed draft manuscript and provided comments, suggestions, and encouragement.

My wife, Mimi, is my chief encourager in all things, including writing. Her loving support enabled me to devote myself to research, writing, and editing on an ongoing basis for three years, while also fulfilling our many family, career, and ministry commitments.

Finally, I must express my gratitude to Christy Wilson himself. Having written his biography, I find myself even more drawn to the one Christy loved so much, even more desirous of a heart for prayer, even more longing to live my life with grace and passion, even more consumed by the wonder of the good news of the cross of Christ, and even more compelled to share that good news with the world around me. For that, I am most grateful.

NOTES

I have relied extensively on personal interviews and emails with the Wilson family, former members of CCCK, and Christy's former students and colleagues at Gordon-Conwell. These sources are mentioned in the acknowledgments.

The Archives of the Billy Graham Center in Wheaton, Illinois, supplied transcripts of hours of taped interviews with Christy while he was alive, as well as old letters, prayer journals, other personal writings, and documents from Princeton, CCCK, and Gordon-Conwell. Readers who want to explore these in greater detail can look up collections 518, the Papers of J. Christy Wilson Jr., and 300, the Records of InterVarsity Christian Fellowship.

Numerous anecdotes and insights in this book depend on Christy's own telling of the stories, which were collected and published in a single volume in *More to Be Desired Than Gold: True Stories Told by Christy Wilson*, comp. Ivan S. Chow, ed. Helen S. Mooradkanian (South Hamilton, MA: Gordon-Conwell Theological Seminary, 1992). The book has gone through several revisions and printings since its original release.

Chapter 8 in this biography originally appeared as "Lost—in an Airplane over Afghanistan!" in *More to Be Desired Than Gold*, 109–13. It is reprinted in its entirety by permission of the Wilson family.

Other published writings by Christy that informed my chapters were *Afghanistan: The Forbidden Harvest* (Elgin, IL: David C. Cook, 1981), now out of print; *Today's Tentmakers: Self-support—An Alternative Model for Worldwide Witness* (Wheaton, IL: Tyndale House, 1979; Eugene, OR: Wipf & Stock, 2002); *One Hundred*

Afghan Persian Proverbs, 4th rev. ed. (Peshawar, Pakistan: Inter-Lit Foundation, 2002); and "Undergirding the Effort with Prayer," *International Journal of Frontier Missions* 11, no. 2 (1994): 61–65.

Details about the 1944 SVM convention, the first InterVarsity missions conference (which birthed the triennial Urbana conference), and the key figures in those events can be found in Keith and Gladys Hunt, *For Christ and the University: The Story of InterVarsity Christian Fellowship of the U.S.A. / 1940–1990* (Downers Grove, IL: InterVarsity Press, 1991); A. Donald MacLeod, *C. Stacey Woods and the Evangelical Rediscovery of the University* (Downers Grove, IL: InterVarsity Press, 2007); and www.urbana.org/history.

Other sources are cited in the footnotes throughout this book.